When Is It Right to Fight?

When Is It Right to Fight?

ROBERT A. MOREY

BETHANY HOUSE PUBLISHERS
MINNEAPOLIS, MINNESOTA 55438
A Division of Bethany Fellowship, Inc.

Published by Bethany House Publishers
A Division of Bethany Fellowship, Inc.
6820 Auto Club Road, Minneapolis, Minnesota 55438

Printed in the United States of America

Library of Congress Cataloging in Publication Data

Morey, Robert A., 1946-
    When is it right to fight?

    Bibliography: p.
    1. War—Religious aspects—Christianity. 2. War—Biblical teaching. I. Title.
BT736.2.M64   1985   241'.6242   85-15708
ISBN 0-87123-810-1 (pbk.)

"If I declare with the loudest voice and clearest exposition every portion of God's truth except for that one little bit which the world and the devil are at the moment attacking, I am not confessing Christ."

Martin Luther

Dr. Morey has received a B.A. in Philosophy, a M.Div. in Theology and a D.Min. in Apologetics. Some of his books have been translated into Spanish, German and Chinese. He is listed in *Contemporary Writers* and the *International Authors and Writers Who's Who*. He is an internationally recognized scholar in the field of apologetics and is presently pastor of New Life Bible Church and Executive Director of the Research and Education Foundation. He has also written:

Death and the Afterlife
Reincarnation and Christianity
Horoscopes and the Christian
How to Answer a Jehovah's Witness
How to Answer a Mormon
A Christian Handbook for Defending the Faith
The Bible and Drug Abuse
The Dooyeweerdian Concept of the Word of God
Worship is all of Life
Is Sunday the Christian Sabbath?
An Examination of Exclusive Psalmody
The Saving Work of Christ
Outlines For Living

Table of Contents

Introduction

"If it is possible,
as far as it depends on you,
live at peace with everyone" (Rom. 12:18).

One of the many evidences of the divine inspiration of the Bible is its practicality. Because there is no conflict between life and doctrine in the Scriptures, we find that our experiences in life correspond exactly to what the Bible said we would experience. God never calls upon us to do what is impossible, impractical or unlivable. Indeed, one of the strongest proofs of the validity of Christianity is that we can live what we believe and believe what we live.

Just because something works does not necessarily mean that it is true, for "the end does not justify the means." Yet, it is equally valid to say that if something is really true, it will work. Hence, the Bible is *true* in the sense that it corresponds to reality. Because it is true, the Bible can be trusted as a safe and practical guide for all of life.

Any doctrine of the Christian life which is not livable or workable on a day-to-day level must be viewed as erroneous on a theoretical level. If we cannot live what we believe, then what we believe must be wrong. If our beliefs are scriptural, then we will find that we can live what we believe. We will bypass the frustration and guilt of unlivable ideas and unattainable goals.

One example of the practicality of God's Word is Paul's

exhortation to the saints at Rome quoted at the beginning of this introduction. There are several things about this exhortation which should be noted.

First, the Apostle is clearly speaking in terms of personal relationships. The context of the chapter concerns the relationship of individual believers to spiritual gifts (vs. 3–8), to inward character qualities (vs. 9–13), to those who persecute them (v. 14), to fellow believers (vs. 15, 16) and to those who offend them (vs. 17–21).

Second, Paul understood that as long as we live in this world, people are going to hurt us. They will fail our expectations and violate our rights. Nowhere does God promise in Scripture that life would be "a bowl of cherries" once we are saved. We are going to be offended and hurt by both Christians and non-Christians. And, from sad personal experience, we must confess that fellow Christians are often more guilty in this area than the typical unbeliever.

Third, Paul is dealing with the fact that we are going to be tempted to render evil for evil, bitterness for bitterness, gossip for gossip, slander for slander, hatred for hatred, etc. Self-preservation is one of the strengths of the human species. But it can be twisted by the depravity of our hearts into a motive for personal vengeance and violence. The desire to "get even" is one of the ugliest human emotions for which no justification can be given.

Fourth, the Christian's response to personal attacks should be to avoid all internal bitterness and external retaliation. We must leave vengeance to the Lord, for He will vindicate us on the Day of Judgment if we have not done anything evil to provoke the animosity or persecution we are experiencing (1 Pet. 4:12–19).

Fifth, while we are called upon to "live at peace with everyone," the Apostle recognizes that this cannot always be done. Therefore he adds, "*If it is possible* . . . live at peace with everyone" (italics mine).

These additional words by the Apostle clearly reveal that there are going to be times when maintaining peace will be impossible, impractical, and unlivable. This is why he qualifies his command with the words "if it is possible."

Notice the practicality of God's Word at this point. God recognizes that we will find ourselves at times in a situation where, although our inner attitude is not motivated by a lust for personal vengeance, peace will not be possible.

Consequently, "peace" cannot always be the Christian response to the evil that men do. There are times when justice must be required and punishment enforced for crimes against the lives and property of others. This is why there is church discipline for the correction or punishment of church members, and civil courts for the prosecution of criminals.

To imagine that the only option given to Christians is peace is to deny the validity of church discipline and civil justice.

To remain undisturbed in the face of repeated or grave evil is not the way of peace because peace is never maintained by giving in to all the demands of evil. For God to expect that attitude would require us to do what is impossible and impractical. It would result in far greater evils.

Sixth, knowing that we would have to find ways of dealing with evil after we have exhausted every avenue of peace, the Apostle moves on in the context to the believer's relationship to civil governments and the civil ethics which guide the actions of the state (Rom. 13:1–7).

The Scriptures always present the view that God established civil government for the good of mankind. In order to promote civil peace and prosperity, God gave certain ethical and moral responsibilities to the state that He denies to individuals. In other words, it is erroneous to assume that all the rules which govern personal ethics should also govern the state. The converse is also true. The rules which govern the actions of the state are not to be taken over by individuals.

For example, while the individual believer or citizen should not use violence to resolve personal conflicts with his fellow Christians or neighbors (Rom. 12:17–19), God has given the state the responsibility of using the sword to punish wrongdoers (Rom. 13:1–7). Or again, while an individual is commanded to love his neighbor even if he is his personal enemy (Matt. 5:44), the state is never commanded by God to love other nations, because governments are not capable of either love or hate. This is why the Old and New Testaments speak of the responsibility of governments in terms of civil *justice*, never love.

The wonderful livability of Scripture is thereby demonstrated by the way Paul dealt with the problem of coping with evil. On a personal level, try to live at peace with everyone. Suffer personal insult and persecution as long as it is possible (Rom. 12:14–21). Go the "second mile" with people (Matt 5:41). Let love cover a multitude of sins (1 Pet. 4:8).

But what should we do if someone will not live at peace with us? If a fellow believer is doing the evil, take the issue to the church for discipline on that sinning member (1 Cor. 5–6). If it is an unbeliever, appeal to the state for justice (Rom. 13:1–7).

That is what Paul did when confronted by a murder plot. He did not hesitate to seek the military protection of the "sword" of the state when his life was in danger (Acts 23:12–35). He clearly saw that while personal insults could be endured by taking the way of peace, when the lives of others or of oneself were in danger, the way of peace had to give way to the way of justice. When peace will no longer work, the use of just force becomes a moral obligation as well as a God-given right.

But, someone may ask, when are we to use force to remedy the evil men do? In what situations is it our moral obligation to recognize with tears that peace is not going to work? When should we seek another solution such as the just use of force? These difficult questions must be addressed by everyone, because we are all confronted at times with evils which demand action and not passivity.

The only way to answer these important questions is to examine the Scriptures to see what God has said to men and women in the past who faced the same issues which we face today. The Scriptures *alone* must lay the foundation for our answers if we are to consider ourselves "Christians" in any sense. Our emotional sensitivities must not be allowed to overrule the Word of God. The opinions of man as to what is moral or immoral in this issue can only be considered where they do not contradict Scripture. We must go to the law and the prophets if we want to see God's answers to the questions surrounding peace and war (Isa. 8:20).

This work is dedicated to those who, with an open mind and heart, will search the Scriptures to discover God's answers to these perplexing problems of life. God's Word promises them that they shall know the truth and the truth shall set them free (John 8:32). To God be the glory.

1

The Law and the Prophets

When we pick up the Bible to investigate any subject, we naturally begin with the Old Testament. In its pages we find the history of the world laid out in terms of God's dealings with mankind in general and with the nation of Israel in particular. As we turn its pages, we find the answers to the great questions of life such as, "Where did we come from?" "Why are we here?" "Where are we going?" "Does life have any meaning?" "Are there any moral absolutes to guide us in life?"

The breathtaking panorama of history recorded in the Old Testament covers thousands of years, and according to the Apostle Paul, it was written for our benefit today (1 Cor. 10:11; Rom. 15:4). Indeed, the New Testament's use of the Old Testament for doctrine (1 Cor. 15:3, 4) and for principles of ethics (1 Cor. 10:1–11) cannot be questioned.

Part of the endless charm of the Old Testament lies in its realistic description of the lives of the patriarchs and prophets. They are pictured with all their faults and weaknesses. This gives us the hope that if God could use them, then He can also use us.

These brave men and women faced the same situations we face today. They had to exercise faith in difficult circumstances. They faced tyrannical governments who were determined not only to rule the whole world, but also to destroy their faith. They had to contend with unemployment, inflation and urban plight. International conflict was frequent. They had to deal with injustice to the poor and oppressed.

Throughout the Old Testament, the patriarchs and prophets are pictured as real people struggling with the same kinds of problems we face today. This is why they are listed in Hebrews 11 as models for us to follow today. In this biblical spirit, let us examine their lives and history for answers to our questions.

GENESIS

Perhaps the best place to begin is with the book of beginnings, Genesis. In its pages we have a record of the origin of all the problems which man has faced in every generation. A brief survey of what Genesis has to say regarding the use of force will be highly instructive.

Spiritual Warfare

Genesis opens with the revelation that a warfare is going on between God and Satan. In the first recorded skirmish on earth, Satan persuades Adam and Eve to join his rebellion against God (Gen. 3:1–16). At the Fall, man became God's enemy and a child of Satan.

This cosmic war between God and Satan now involves the inhabitants of the earth as well as those of heaven. God is called the "Lord of Hosts," i.e., "the Lord of armies." He is the Lord of the armies in heaven and on earth.

Throughout Scripture, earthly wars, where the conflict is clearly between good and evil, are viewed as manifestations of the spiritual conflict taking place in heaven. For example, in Job 1:6–17, the Sabeans and Chaldeans, as agents of Satan in his conflict with God, raided Job's flocks and killed his servants. The violence against Job was a reflection of the war between God and Satan. Other Old Testament examples can be cited: 1 Chron. 21:1; 2 Kings 6:8–18; Dan. 10:7–14.

The New Testament continues the tradition of depicting the course of human history as warfare between God and

Satan, viewing it in terms of conflict between two kingdoms (Acts 26:18; Col. 1:13).

Heavenly and earthly warfare will never be halted until Christ returns to earth to judge the wicked and establish His eternal kingdom (Isa. 65:17–25; Matt. 24:6–8).

The last battle which shall end all wars will involve both heavenly and earthly armies (Rev. 12:7–9; 19:11–21). This last battle is what the Bible calls Armageddon (Rev. 16:15, 16).

Some sincere people are very hopeful and optimistic that a permanent international peace can be achieved through treaties, disarmament, good will, the United Nations, or one-world government. The United Nations building in New York City has engraved on its walls: "They shall beat their swords into plowshares, and their spears into pruning hooks . . ." (Isa. 2:4). It was assumed that the passage quoted referred to a permanent peace achievable through human means in this age.

But Isaiah is only saying that wars will cease after Christ returns and judges the wicked (Isa. 2:10–21). Isaiah is describing the new earth where righteousness reigns (vs. 1–3).

In the New Testament, Jesus clearly indicated that wars will continue until the end of history (Matt. 24:6, 7).

In this light, only the most extreme utopian idealist could possibly believe that man will be able to abolish all wars without the intervention of God.

What is a utopian idealist? Someone who is in love with an idea which when put into practice will produce the exact opposite of what the idea was supposed to accomplish.

For example, some idealists sincerely believe that if the Soviets invaded the United States, the Americans could step into the streets with signs saying "We love you," and by offering their hand of friendship, they would not be run down by the Soviet tanks, but the Russians would in turn offer their hands in friendship. The United States could use the same techniques of nonviolent resistance that Ghandi used on the British.[1]

---

[1] R. Sider and R. Taylor, *Nuclear Holocaust and Christian Hope* (Downers Grove, Ill.: InterVarsity Press, 1982), p. 275.

There are several problems with this kind of idealism.

First, the thousands of people who have been crushed under the treads of Soviet tanks in Hungary, Czechoslovakia, Indochina, Afghanistan, Africa, Cuba, and Central America establish that Soviet tank crews have no moral difficulty whatsoever in running innocent people down. Historical reality simply does not correspond to romantic ideas.

Second, the tactics used by Ghandi, such as passive resistance, hunger strikes and work strikes, worked on the British government because they were dealing with a democratic nation whose sense of basic morality would not allow the slaughter of thousands of innocent men, women and children.[2]

While passive resistance worked in a democratic context, such tactics have never worked in ruthless totalitarian government such as the Soviet government, which has no moral restraints at all. One can think of the five million men, women and children murdered by the Communists in the Ukraine. Even Ghandi stated that passive resistance would not work with Hitler.[3]

In the twentieth century, some people sincerely believe that our only hope lies in a one-world government. All international wars will cease because there won't be any national governments left to fight each other. If we could have just one government and one religion for the whole world, all would be peaceful.

The noted infidel Bertrand Russell argued that regardless of the fact that such a world government would necessarily be molded after the totalitarian model of Hitler's Third Reich or Stalin's reign of terror, the loss of individual freedom would be more than compensated for by the absence of international war and the avoidance of nuclear war. Russell became well known for his "Better red than dead" position.

Several things immediately come to mind in response to the idea of a one-world government solving mankind's problems.

---

[2]R. Grenier, *The Gandhi Nobody Knows* (Thomas Nelson, 1983) pp. 67ff.
[3]Ibid.

First, the biblical authors were realistic, not idealistic, about the nature of man. As you read the record of man's inhumanity to man described in the pages of Scripture, you must come to the conclusion that man is sinful, violent, and selfish. Nothing will ever change this fact until Christ returns. Until then, there will be rape, murder, theft, and war. Until then, nations will fight nations over real estate, wealth, and energy resources. Governments will have to use force in order to keep violent criminals in place. Moral persuasion will not work as long as evil men walk on the earth.

In opposition to the rugged realism of the Scriptures, the following statements are examples of an unrealistic view of human nature and history. They reflect an idealistic stance toward the Soviet Union. We have heard these statements countless times in both secular and Christian colleges, when war and peace have been discussed.

"The Russians are no different from us than anyone else."

"The Russians do not want war but peace."

"The Communists are armed only as a defense against the threat of the West."

"The Communists do not want to conquer the world."

"If the Soviets invaded, we could stand in front of their tanks with signs saying, 'Smile, God loves you' and reach out our hands in friendship."

"Since violence breeds violence, our use of nonviolence will result in nonviolence. Instead of running us over, the Soviet soldiers and their tanks will greet us with flowers instead of bullets."

"We should sign a treaty with the Soviets to disarm totally even if they will not allow us on-site verification of their disarmament. We can trust them because they have humanity's welfare at heart. We can trust them to keep their word."

We cannot imagine saying such nonsense to the more than one hundred million people slaughtered by the Marxists in this century. How could anyone make these statements while looking at the captive nations in Europe, the brutal assault upon Afghanistan, the use of Soviet weapons to fan war and revolution in Asia, Africa, and Central America, and the brutal shooting down of a Korean commercial airplane full of innocent men, women, and children on August 31, 1983?

Second, the Bible teaches that Satan will create a one-world government in the last days before Christ returns. The Antichrist will head up a one-world government which will make Hitler's concentration camps look like a Sunday school picnic (Rev. 13–18).

Third, when we say that the Communists are evil and inspired by Satan, we are simply speaking in the spirit of biblical truth. One of the fundamental teachings of Marxism is that God does not exist. Any system founded on this belief will receive the support of Satan who hates us.

The Apostle Paul tells us that the presence of the Spirit of God brings liberty (2 Cor. 3:17). *Wherever* the Spirit of God is present, there will be liberty.

In opposition to this, the presence of Satan always means bondage, oppression, and tyranny (Luke 13:10–16). A realist must admit that Marxism has never produced freedom. It has an unbroken track record of violent oppression and tyranny.

Whenever the people in a Communist country are allowed to vote with their feet, they escape to the West for freedom. In his book *Inside the Soviet Army*, Suvorov says the Communists know that their people would escape if given the chance. This is why they have surrounded their borders with high walls, electric fences, mine fields, goon squads, killer dogs, and machine gun posts.

The Soviets know that as long as the West is free, the enslaved peoples of the world have hope—hope that perhaps the West will one day deliver them from the tyranny and oppression they are under; hope that by some means they may escape to the West for freedom and opportunity.

In order to destroy this hope for freedom, the Communist tyrants must destroy the West. As long as there is a place of freedom left on earth, their reign of darkness is in peril.

This is why, says Suvorov, it is simplistic to believe that the Soviets will be content to coexist peaceably with the West. Coexistence has always been viewed by the Soviets as a tool for the destruction of the West.

Fourth, let us be thankful that God does not sit idly by while Satan violently destroys the innocent. God's angelic armies do not use the techniques of nonresistance in their fight against Satan. Instead, God's army will forcefully cast them out of heaven at the final battle. If pacifism does not work in heaven, neither will it work on earth.

Capital Punishment

The death penalty for such serious crimes as murder is clearly taught in the Old Testament. The death penalty was first introduced in the garden of Eden as the ultimate punishment for man's sin (Gen. 2:17). It was the focal point of Satan's attack on Eve (Gen. 3:4). He assured her that God would not really carry out the punishment of capital punishment ("You will not really die"). It was a part of the consciousness of Cain (Gen. 4:8, 13–15) and was reinstated by God himself after the Flood, when God and man began their relationship all over again (Gen. 9:6).

It is viewed throughout the Old Testament as being a just punishment for serious civil crimes. It is never viewed as being cruel, unusual, unjust, or unloving. It was God's love of truth, justice, and His own people that led Him to establish capital punishment. Capital punishment safeguards the harmony of any society.

Capital punishment in the Old Testament is based upon the fact that man was made in the image of God. Capital punishment thus rests upon a high view of man in which it is recognized that there is a basic qualitative difference between killing a human being and an animal. A man is the image-bearer of God, and to kill a man is so horrendous that the death of the murderer is the only thing that can possibly satisfy the demands of justice.

The New Testament also recognizes the justice of the death penalty (Matt. 21:40, 41; Rom. 1:32; Rom. 13:4). Without the death penalty as part of Jewish law, Christ could not have died for our sins. Without the death of Christ, no salvation was possible. The death penalty was the means God used to provide salvation for sinners.

At no point in the Old or New Testaments is the death penalty removed or withdrawn. Its application by the state is made one of the marks of a God-ordained government in Rom. 13:4. Christ himself could speak of its application on an international level without any hint of condemnation (Matt. 21:40, 41). It is never viewed as being intrinsically immoral, unjust, or wrong.

But, one might ask, what does the Bible's sanction of the death penalty have to do with the subject of war? The death penalty is a just punishment for whatever number of criminals are involved in the perpetration of a crime.

If five men acting in a group murder one victim, all five men deserve to die. The death penalty can thus be legitimately applied to armies which are invading, raping, robbing, looting, and killing. It makes no difference in principle whether an army or an individual is guilty.

That is why God ordered the destruction of entire cities such as Sodom. The inhabitants of those wicked cities deserved to die because of the heinous crimes they were commiting. When Israel conquered Canaan, it was simply applying the death penalty on a national level.

Once we admit the justice of killing a murderer for his crime, then, in principle, we will have to admit the justice of destroying an entire army.

We must also point out that the ethics employed on the Judgment Day give us the biblical explanation for such things as the Flood, the destruction of Sodom and Gomorrah, the genocide of the Canaanites, the dispersion of Israel, and the destruction of the temple in A.D. 70.

Each of these events were understood by the biblical authors to be "previews of coming attractions" on the Judgment Day. The various holocausts described in the Old and New Testaments were simply intrusions of Judgment Day ethics into present history to give us a sneak preview of what that day will be like.

That is why Jesus himself could refer to the holocaust of

the Flood (Matt. 24:36–39), the fiery destruction of Sodom and Gomorrah (Luke 17:24–35), and even the destruction of the temple (Matt. 24:1–3) as being eschatological intrusions of the Judgment Day ethic into present history to pre-picture what the Judgment Day will be like. The apostles viewed such holocausts as eschatological pictures of the judgment when Christ returns (2 Pet. 2:4–3:7; Jude 6, 7).

One of the pillars of the just-war theory is the eschatological justice and righteousness of the final holocaust and the fact that the ethics of that final war have intruded into human history again and again in order to warn man of coming judgment. There is thus an eschatological basis to the just-war theory that most people have never considered.

In addition to its eschatological basis, the just-war theory also has Christological foundation. If the Scriptures taught that the use of force is intrinsically wrong and immoral, how could it describe the return of Christ as Jesus waging a righteous war?

> And I saw heaven opened; and behold, a white horse, and He who sat upon it is called Faithful and True; and in righteousness He judges and wages war (Rev. 19:11, NASB).

The fact that Jesus will return to punish the wicked with flaming fire reveals that the use of force is not intrinsically incompatible with love, justice, righteousness, or truth. As long as the war to end all wars is righteous and true, lesser wars fought for the same reasons will always be righteous and true. Once the righteousness of Armageddon is accepted, the principle of the just war is established.

The First Recorded Just War (Gen. 14)

The first recorded use of force in a just-war context is Abraham's "slaughter of Chedorlaomer and the kings that were with him, at the Valley of Shaveh" (Gen. 14:17, KJV).

The facts of the situation are quite simple and straightforward. An invading army had defeated and looted Sodom and Gomorrah and taken Lot and his family captive. When Abraham heard this, he armed 318 of his servants and pursued the enemy until they reached Dan. He divided his servants into two groups, attacking from both sides under the cover of darkness. Chedorlaomer was defeated and all the captive people freed.

There are several important things for us to notice.

First, Moses describes Abraham's actions with obvious pride over Abraham's demonstration of courage and love for his fellow man. In Moses' account there is no sense of disgust or grief over Abraham's use of force.

Second, there was no divine command given or needed for Abraham to know that as his "brother's keeper," he had to deliver Lot. It was obviously just and righteous for Abraham to use force in such a situation. If he would have stood idly by and refused to help Lot in his time of need, he would have been branded a heartless coward or scoundrel for the rest of his life.

Third, some people have mistakenly thought that only wars in the Old Testament which were directly initiated and commanded by God can be viewed as just. All other wars must be viewed as sinful. How can one respond to this idea?

Consider Abraham, whose own sense of justice initiated the use of force. However, after he returned, God put His stamp of approval on Abraham's actions by having Melchizidek, the high priest, bless him (Gen. 14:18–20).

The New Testament's approval of Melchizidek's blessing of Abraham and the fact that Melchizidek is viewed as a type of Christ prevents anyone from saying that Melchizidek's blessing was not a divine blessing (Heb. 7:1–3).

Fourth, it is assumed by some that only wars fought in self-defense are just. It would be immoral for one nation to attack another nation unless that nation was attacked first.

The problem with the above theory is that Abraham's use of force was not in self-defense. Chedorlaomer was not attacking him. Abraham was initiating the conflict by pursuing and attacking a tyrannical enemy.

In this light, it is clear that wars of aggression in which one strikes the first blow against tyrants can sometimes be viewed as perfectly just and righteous.

It was perfectly just and proper for the Free World to go to war against Hitler and Japan. The U.N. was right when it entered Korea to stop the Communists. When surrounding African nations overthrew Idi Amin's reign of terror, this was just and right. The people of Grenada rejoiced when a united force of Caribbean and U.S. troops came into their country and delivered them from Communist oppression.

It can also be legitimately deduced from Abraham's example that it is perfectly just for the Free World to use force when necessary and practical to deliver captive nations everywhere (Estonia, Lithuania, Poland, Czechoslovakia, Afghanistan, East Germany, Angola, Cuba, Central America, etc.).

Abraham's aggressive use of force to deliver his brothers from tyranny and enslavement justifies all other wars fought for the same reason. One of our greatest sins today is that the West is not more actively involved in funding freedom fighters everywhere from Cuba to Afghanistan. The West is failing to be a Good Samaritan to our poor oppressed brothers who are being crushed under the heels of Marxist tyranny.

If the West would only follow Abraham's godly example, the Communists would soon abandon their program for world conquest. The oppressed people in every Communist country, if given the funds and weapons, would rise up and overthrow their slave masters.

Let us not forget that in the Hungarian and Czechoslovakian revolts, when the oppressed peoples rose up against their Marxist masters, they cried out to the West for military help. To our shame, the West refused to give them help, and the freedom fighters were crushed under the tracks of Soviet tanks. The sin of the West in not going to the aid of their brothers in distress is one of the most shameful and cowardly chapters in Western history.

The First Treaty

Lest anyone accuse Abraham of being a bloodthirsty and violent man, the first treaty recorded in Scripture which avoided war was between Abraham and the Philistines (Gen. 21:22–33).

The treaty lessened tensions between Abraham and Abimilech and avoided war over water and grazing rights. Isaac later re-ratified this treaty because it had worked to keep peace in the area (Gen. 26:26–33).

In the light of this passage, it is clear that whenever differences can be worked out by negotiations and treaty, this is the proper thing to do. The just-war theory has no lust for war or violence. We should try to avoid war by negotiation, compromise, and treaties. War is always the last resort. It should be an option only after *all* other means have failed.

It is also clear that Abraham was a man of peace. His servants were not normally armed (Gen. 14:14). He negotiated treaties wherever possible and went to war only when there was no other option left open.

Unjust violence

Scripture is clear in its approval of the just use of force by parents to discipline their children, by the police to punish criminals, and by a nation to protect its citizens. On the other hand, Scripture is equally clear in its condemnation of the personal use of unjust violence in taking the life of innocent people. The Scriptures recognize a fundamental difference between the use of just force and the exercise of personal violence.

The first recorded instance of personal violence was Cain's murder of Abel (Gen. 4:8–15). In no sense can Cain's actions be justified. Later, Lamech, the father of polygamy, is portrayed as a wicked man who boasted of plural murders (Gen. 4:23).

Perhaps the clearest example of unjust violence is found in Genesis 34 where Shechem rapes Dinah and then has the gall to ask for her hand in marriage (vs. 1–12).

Jacob's sons, acting on their own without the advice or consent of their father, tricked all the men of Shechem's village into being circumcised (vs. 13–17). Then two of the brothers,

Simeon and Levi, attacked the city while the men were still incapacitated and murdered all the males (vs. 25–26). The other brothers rushed in and looted the village and enslaved the women and children (vs. 27–29).

When Jacob was told of what his sons had done, particularly Simeon and Levi, he cried out against this obviously unjustifiable act of violence (v. 30).

Several things can be deduced from this passage.

First, since Shechem alone was guilty, he alone should have been punished. Killing all the men in his village was unjustifiable as there is no indication they were involved in the rape.

Second, the sons of Jacob acted out of "great anger" (v. 7) instead of a concern for justice or truth. The use of violence for personal vengeance is condemned in the Old Testament (Deut. 32:35) as well as in the New Testament (Rom. 12:19). The just-war theory does not attempt to justify such acts of violence.

When the New Testament condemns acts of personal violence in such places as Rom. 12:19, it is merely quoting the Old Testament's condemnation. The Old Testament's censure of personal violence in such places as Deut. 32:35 is not viewed as a condemnation of the just use of force elsewhere in the Old Testament. It is clear that while acts of vindictive personal violence are never justified, the proper use of force is justifiable.

Third, Jacob clearly sensed that the action of his sons was so unjust that even the immoral Philistines would be outraged at such injustice (Gen. 34:30).

Lastly, Jacob warned his sons that such acts of violence would only lead to further acts of violence. While the just use of force can solve problems as it did for Abraham, the unjust use of violence may create more violence.

EXODUS

The earliest account of active resistance to a tyrannical state is found in Ex. 1:15–22. Pharaoh had commanded the midwives to kill each newborn Hebrew boy. The midwives "feared God" and disobeyed the king. One example of such resistance was the hiding of Moses for three months and then his concealment in the bullrushes (Ex. 2:1–3).

Moses clearly praises the midwives for fearing God more than fearing the king. When the choice was between obedience to God or to a tyrannical power, God had to be obeyed. This is taught in the New Testament (Acts 5:29).

Whenever the state commands something which violates God's law, that government has entered into an area for which it has no divine warrant. It is therefore devoid of any valid authority at that point, and we can ignore or resist it with God's blessing. It has become tyranny and not true government.

The true nature of tyranny is never so clear as when it mandates the killing of innocent children, born or unborn. There is thus a direct parallel between the atrocities of the Egyptians in Moses' day and the population-control abortion policies of the Communist Chinese.

Since the Hebrews were unarmed, God himself used force to deliver them. He used the force of the ten plagues to secure their release from tyranny and oppression. The many deaths resulting from the plagues and the slaughter of Pharaoh's army in the Red Sea all reflect God's just use of force as a means to throw the yoke of tyranny off the neck of His people.

After God's people were safe from further attack, He gave them civil, ceremonial, and cultic laws to regulate their lives. If God wanted His people to be pacifists, this would have been an ideal time to establish this. Instead, God revealed the death penalty as His way to punish violent criminals (Ex. 21). Lesser crimes warranted lesser punishments (Ex. 22).

NUMBERS

Then the Lord spoke to Moses in the wilderness of Sinai, in the tent of meeting, on the first of the second month, in the second year after they had come out of the land of Egypt saying, 'Take a census of all the congregation of the sons of Israel, by their families, by their fathers' households, according to the number of names, every male, head by head from twenty years old and upward, whoever is able to go out to war in Israel, you and Aaron shall number them by their armies' (Num. 1:1–3, NASB).

God initiates the numbering of the males in Israel twenty years old and up in order to draft an army. While God delivered them out of Egypt by His own hand, He now wanted them to wage war by their own hands. They could not hope to maintain the freedoms God had given them except by the use of force. Thus Israel developed an army at God's command.

From this passage, it is clear that a military draft is perfectly just and necessary for the maintenance of freedom and for protection against one's enemies. The pacifist's contention that drafting men for military service is somehow intrinsically immoral or unjust is at once refuted by the simple fact that it was God himself who initiated the military draft.

Let it also be noted that God never said to draft the women of Israel. The drafting of women is an unjustifiable intrusion into the sovereign sphere of the family for which Scripture gives no warrant or precedent.

JOSHUA

Joshua's leadership in military, as well as spiritual matters, will stand as a shining example of the warrior priest. As a Spirit-filled believer (Deut. 34:9), Joshua led his people to victory over the enemies of God and Israel.

Let it not be forgotten that the annihilation of the Canaanites was an eschatological holocaust prefiguring the Day of Judgment. The sins of the Canaanites had reached the point where justice demanded their destruction. Thus, it was said that their sin had "ripened" or "filled out" to the point where judgment had to come (Gen. 15:16; Josh. 11:20; 1 Kings 21:26; Matt. 23:32).

Peace was won and maintained by the use of force (Josh. 21:44–45). This was true for Israel and has been true for every nation throughout human history. Only the wise use of force can establish and maintain peace.

JUDGES

In this book, we have the history of the freedom fighters God raised up to overthrow tyrannical powers. These brave men and women used assassinations, terrorist acts, sabotage, guerrilla warfare, and open revolt by armed resistance, all under the blessing of God. At no point in Judges are these freedom fighters condemned because they used force to destroy tyranny. Instead, they are described in glowing terms as heroes. Let it also be noted that the authors of the New Testament do not hesitate to hold up these same freedom fighters as examples of faith and courage for modern-day Christians to follow (Heb. 11:32–40).

If the New Testament taught pacifism, as some imagine, the freedom fighters described in Judges would never have been praised by the New Testament writers as examples to follow today.

Tyrants oppressed Israel because the Israelites failed to carry out God's command to annihilate the Canaanites (Judg. 1–2) and because they became involved in idolatry (Judg. 3:7–8). They were oppressed by one tyrannical power after another and they experienced peace only under the freedom fighters or judges that God raised up to deliver them.

God's people used open-armed rebellion to overthrow tyranny only when there was a reasonable hope of winning. When there was no possibility of success, the people submitted to oppression and waited until the circumstances changed.

On other occasions, when they were not able to launch an open revolution due to a lack of weapons (1 Sam. 13:19) or due to the presence of superior forces, they carried on guerrilla warfare tactics to harass the tyrants.

The following chart illustrates how God's freedom fighters overthrew tyrannical powers in their day. It clearly shows that the Scriptures never view a tyrannical power as a legitimate government. Just because an elite group was in power because of their weapons, they were not viewed as the government ordained of God, because God never ordains tyranny. Thus, God never commands His people to view tyranny as valid authority.

THE JUDGES AND THE TYRANTS

TYRANT	FREEDOM FIGHTERS	METHODS USED	TIME OF PEACE
1. Mesopotamia (8 years)	Othniel (3:9)	Armed Revolt	40 yrs.
2. Moab (18 years)	Ehud (3:15)	Assassination Armed Revolt	80 yrs.
3. Philistines	Shamgar (3:31)	Armed Revolt	—
4. Hazor (20 years)	Deborah/Barak (4:4, 6)	Assassination Armed Revolt	40 yrs.
5. Media (7 years)	Gideon (6:11)	Armed Revolt	40 yrs.
6. Abimelech (3 years)	A Woman (9:53)	Assassination Armed Revolt	—
7. Philistines (18 years)	Jephthah (11:1)	Armed Revolt	6 yrs.
8. Philistines (40 years)	Samson (14:1)	Assassination, Sabotage, Guerrilla Warfare	—

1 SAMUEL—2 CHRONICLES

God is revealed in 1 Samuel as "the Lord of Armies" (1 Sam. 1:3), because force had to be exercised by God's prophets, princes, priests, and people to resist tyranny.

The just use of force against tyranny was exercised by Samuel (1 Sam. 15:32, 33), Saul (1 Sam. 11:11), Jonathan (1 Sam. 14:13), David (1 Sam. 17:41–51), Solomon (1 Kings 9:22), Elijah (1 Kings 18:40), Elisha (2 Kings 2:23–25), Jehu (2 Kings 9), Joash (2 Kings 11), and many others.

Let it be noted that the government which was in power at the time was not necessarily the government God had appointed. Thus, there would often be two governments functioning at the same time—illegitimate tyrannical power in office and a legitimate divinely appointed government in exile.

The tyrannical power was viewed as illegitimate, and it could be resisted and overthrown by the use of force. For example, even though Athaliah headed the government then in power, she was overthrown because the government actually belonged to Joash (2 Kings 11).

When Athaliah was overthrown, she claimed that it was "treason" (2 Kings 11:14). But her overthrow and death were viewed by the biblical prophets as justice and not treason, because tyranny is never a divinely appointed form of government. Tyranny is always the usurpation of appointed government.

It should also be noted that the use of assassination to remove tyrants is viewed in Scripture as thoroughly just and commendatory. Ehud's assassination of Eglon or the other assassinations committed by freedom fighters to overthrow tyrants throughout biblical history are always praised in Scripture as a legitimate and just means of force. If one takes the biblical record seriously, assassination to remove a tyrant is not murder.

In this light, we must praise Deitrich Bonhoeffer's involvement in an assassination plot against Hitler. If the plot had succeeded, WW II would have been concluded early and many thousands of lives would have been saved.

One modern example of a tyrannical power is the Soviet dictatorship. The Russian people never chose these tyrants to be in power and they would overthrow them if they had the opportunity. Aleksander Solzhenitsyn has clearly demonstrated that the Russian people are the oppressed victims of an illegitimate tyrannical power. The same is true for the oppressed peoples in all captive nations. The tyranny that is oppressing them is not ordained of God and is to be overthrown whenever possible.

One cannot but wonder what wonderful blessings would have been bestowed on humanity if such tyrants as Lenin, Stalin, Mao, Hitler, and Mussolini had been assassinated or if modern-day tyrants were removed by assassination. Certainly the oppressed people whom they are victimizing would rejoice at the fall of these evil men.

EZRA—NEHEMIAH

The just use of force is illustrated in these two books. The people of God returned to Israel by decree of King Cyrus (Ezra

1). They obtained a legal right to rebuild Jerusalem. Later, under King Artaxerxes, their building permit was revoked (Ezra 4). Because of the overwhelming numbers of their enemies and the superior forces of Artaxerxes, the Jews ceased building Jerusalem.

Fourteen years later, Nehemiah's petition to Artaxerxes to rebuild the city was granted (Neh. 2). With the influx of Nehemiah's group, they now had enough people to use force to defend themselves (Neh. 4). The city and the temple were completed because the people were on constant military alert. Half the workers acted as heavily armed sentries. The other half worked with one hand and carried a sword in the other or kept one strapped to their waists. The city would not have been built otherwise.

THE PSALMS AND ECCLESIASTES

The imprecatory Psalms are the cries of oppressed people against the evils of tyranny. The just death of such tyrants is viewed as an eschatological judgment reflecting the ethics of the Judgment Day itself.

Throughout the Psalms, the people of God are told that they should hate tyranny with all of their hearts because God hates it (Ps. 139:19–22). God is called upon to destroy those who oppress the poor and needy (Ps. 12). The death of tyrants is righteous and just (Ps. 28).

There is not a single psalm which teaches nonresistance to tyranny. The Psalms were written by men who believed that the death of tyrants is the just judgment of God.

In Ecclesiastes, we have the opinion of the wisest man who ever lived. In Eccles. 3:8, Solomon states, "There is a time for war and a time for peace." We would not expect to find any other opinion from such a realistic and wise man as Solomon. Throughout human history there will always be a time for war and a time for peace.

THE PROPHETS

In all the condemnations listed against Israel by the prophets, not once is the use of force for personal or civil defense denounced as sin. On the other hand, we find that prophets such as Amos denounced tyranny, and Jeremiah denounced the oppression of the poor (Amos 2:6–8; 4:1–3; Jer. 22:13–27).

The people are condemned for not stopping the tyrants from robbing widows and orphans and oppressing the poor. The prophets were concerned that no one was doing anything about the tyranny which was oppressing the people. This wickedness led to God's judgment on the nation.

While wars will cease when the Messiah comes and sets up the eternal kingdom (Isa. 2:1–5; 65:17–25), God has not told us to live in this wicked world as if we were already living in the eternal kingdom where the lion and the lamb shall lie down together. What will work one day in the context of perfection and sinlessness will not work now in the context of sinfulness where the lion devours the lamb.

CONCLUSION

In our survey of the Old Testament, we have found that from Genesis to Malachi, God views the use of force to deal with tyranny and crime as just, holy and true. The Bible portrays freedom fighting as a reflection of God's justice and is therefore an aspect of the image-bearing capacity of man.

While we must avoid all acts of personal violence, the use of force to overthrow tyranny is blessed and sanctioned by God himself. People have the moral obligation to take whatever action is necessary to fight for the freedom and liberty of all the oppressed peoples of the world.

FOR REVIEW AND DISCUSSION

1. Do you think the Old Testament is relevant today? Should we apply it to such modern issues as pacifism?
2. Did Jesus or the Apostles use the Old Testament to establish morality or doctrines? What implications can be drawn from this?
3. If something is morally right or wrong in one age, can we assume that it will be morally the same in other ages? For

example, in the Old Testament, adultery was viewed as morally wrong. Is adultery ever right? Similarly, in the Old Testament, the use of force is viewed as morally right. Can someone rightfully say that the use of force is wrong today because we live in a different age? Could the New Testament view something as morally wrong if it was viewed as morally right in the Old Testament?

4. Given Abraham's example in Gen. 14, is the use of force justified to punish evil doers and to deliver people who are oppressed? Did he have to wait for a special call from heaven or did his own sense of justice tell him to fight for Lot's deliverance? Did God approve of his actions?

5. What is the difference between the use of force and an act of violence?

2

Jesus and the Gospels

It would be difficult to overstate the importance of the Gospels. In the pages of Matthew, Mark, Luke and John we find the matchless words and life of the Lord Jesus. No literature, ancient or modern, can ever excel the beauty and depth of the words of Jesus, who spoke as no other man has ever spoken. The Gospels will be forever loved and enjoyed by God's people. In their pages we see Jesus in all the dignity of His perfect humanity and the glory of His work of salvation.

As we approach the Gospel material, we must emphasize the necessity of not reading into the Bible ideas and issues which are uniquely related to the twentieth century. Instead, the only valid hermeneutical assumption we can make is that Jesus and the apostles will deal primarily with the issues and questions of their first-century audience. We should not expect them to deal with such things as nuclear weapons because such things did not exist in their day.

This means we cannot claim direct Gospel support for issues which could not have been of any interest in the first century, because they did not yet exist. We can easily fall into the trap of getting more out of the Bible than what is really there.

An honest reading of the Gospels reveals that neither Jesus nor His apostles ever deal directly with such modern abstract issues as the morality of war, nuclear weapons, unilateral disarmament, foreign and domestic policy, industrial pollution or urban blight. Nowhere do they directly answer such questions as:

"What is our responsibility in times of war?"

"Is it proper for a nation to go to war?"

"Should the police carry weapons?"

Once this point is understood, it becomes obvious that the only way for us to arrive at answers to some of these issues and questions is to deduce by logical inference what Jesus might have said if He had been asked about such things.

We readily admit that logical deductions can be tricky. We must be very careful not to put our words into the mouth of the Lord Jesus. All we can do is arrive at His most probable answers. We must base our research on logical inferences drawn from His sermons and the way He dealt with problems in His own day.

Once we understand that the best we can come up with is the most probable answer drawn from inference, we must be careful to avoid arguing in a circle. Many stumble into this typical violation of logic quite sincerely, and quite blindly.

For example, what if we approached the Gospels with the assumption that we already knew that Jesus was a pacifist before even picking up the Bible to see what He said? We would naturally give a biased interpretation of His words in such passages as the Sermon on the Mount.

Once we had done this, we could then argue that Jesus was a pacifist on the basis of His words. Proving in our conclusion what we had already assumed in our premise, we would end up arguing in a circle.

This equally applies to someone who uses circular reasoning to prove that Jesus was in favor of war. If the form of the argument is invalid, it is invalid no matter which position is using it.

Since we can only infer what Jesus might have said about such things as national wars, we must accept the answer which has the most evidence. We cannot make a "leap of faith" as some do and arbitrarily assume that our position is the biblical one simply because we wish it to be so.

THE MOST PROBABLE ANSWER

At no point in Jesus' ministry did He ever tell Israel or Rome that governments should disarm. He never condemned the just use of force as taught in the Scriptures, nor did He ever condemn the police for using force to punish criminals. Despite the clarity of the Old Testament in its divine approval of the use of force, Jesus never once preached against a nation having an army or the state maintaining a police force.

Logically, this can lead us to only one possible inference. Jesus' silence meant that He approved of and accepted the Old Testament precedent of the valid use of force. Whenever we study the Scriptures, a biblical and historical precedent stands until directly removed by divine revelation.

The following points from the Gospels further strengthen this logical inference:

1. Jesus spoke with obvious approval of a king who waged a just war to punish a wicked people by putting them to death (Matt. 21:33–41). While Jesus was not discussing war *per se*, His use of a just-war model for this parable is possible only if Jesus accepted the Old Testament concept of the just use of force.

2. When dealing with Roman or Jewish soldiers, Jesus never told them to leave the military or that it was morally wrong to be soldiers (Matt. 8:5–13; Luke 6:15). This lends further support to the inference that Jesus accepted the scriptural position of the valid use of force. If He were a pacifist and opposed in principle any violence by anyone, He would not have failed to rebuke those who were in the military. Jesus was not known for overlooking sin in the lives of those who sat under His teaching. He denounced sin wherever and in whomever He saw it.

3. In Matt. 24:6, 7, Jesus clearly stated that wars would remain part of human experience until the end of the age. If He were a pacifist, then this would have been a perfect opportunity to condemn all wars. Jesus did not do so in this passage. This underscores the fact that although Jesus referred to the use of force in war or self-defense on many oc-

casions, not once did He condemn such things.

4. Since the people of God had been involved in political and military life throughout history (Abraham, Joshua and Daniel, for example), the fact that Jesus never once told His disciples that they could no longer be involved in those spheres of life is significant.

5. One searches in vain for a secular/sacred dichotomy in Jesus' teaching. To Him all of life was sacred. His disciples were involved in every walk of life. Jesus did not condemn governmental or military careers as being "secular" or sinful.

Once we understand that Jesus Christ is Lord of all life and all life has been sanctified by His dominion, the secular/sacred dichotomy is destroyed. There is no occupation or area in life which a child of God may not be involved in as long as it is not in violation of God's moral law as given in Scripture.

6. Jesus said in John 18:36 that if His church were an earthly kingdom, it would be perfectly proper for His disciples to take up weapons and fight for Him.

While Jesus is clearly, in this passage, forbidding the church as an institution to use physical force in its discipline or defense, He clearly states here that an earthly kingdom can and should fight when necessary.

7. In His parables, Jesus often pictured rulers using valid force to punish wrongdoers (Matt. 18:23–35; 21:38–41; 22:13, etc.). While this is compatible with the teaching of the Old Testament on the just use of force, Jesus would never have given such parables if He were a pacifist. This logically implies that Jesus carried on the teaching of the Old Testament.

8. When the Jews brought Jesus to Pilate, they claimed that Jesus was trying to overthrow the Roman government (Luke 23:1–5). While it is clear that the Jews were wrong in saying Jesus had come to start a violent revolution, it is equally clear that such an accusation could never have been used against Jesus if He had been publicly preaching pacifism.

9. At the beginning and the end of His ministry, Jesus used just force to cleanse the temple (Matt. 21:12; John 2:15). His whip of cords and the Greek words used to describe His driving out the money-changers (drove, poured out, over-

threw) cannot be legitimately interpreted to mean anything else than a forcible ejection of the money-changers. The only logical inference possible is that Jesus condoned the just use of force.

When the Apostle John described this episode in Jesus' life, he recorded that the disciples appealed to an Old Testament passage as a justification of Christ's use of force (John 2:17). This demonstrates beyond all doubt that the disciples were not pacifists.

10. Throughout His ministry, Jesus spoke of His using force on the Day of Judgment to punish rebellious sinners (Matt. 25:41, 46). If the sinless Son of God is going to use force to destroy His enemies, then it is not possible to view the use of force as being intrinsically wrong or immoral. We must therefore conclude that force is right in some situations.

11. When Jesus' enemies tried to capture Him, He demonstrated that no one could take His life away from Him (John 10:17, 18). Jesus exercised divine force and knocked down His attackers (John 18:1–6). Since the Son of God himself exercised force in self-defense, then the use of force in self-defense should be viewed as good.

12. Jesus told His disciples to buy weapons to arm themselves (Luke 22:36–38). While this is hardly consistent with a pacifist picture of Jesus, it does strengthen the inference that Jesus approved of the Old Testament principle of the use of weapons in self-defense. We cannot imagine a pacifist arming his disciples with weapons.

13. After Peter had cut off Malchus' ear, Jesus did not tell Peter to throw away his sword but to put it back in its sheath. Evidently there would be other occasions where it could be rightfully used (John 18:11).

God's plan of salvation called for Christ to die. The disciples would have hindered God's plan if they had risen up to fight for Christ and delivered Him from the Jews. When force is exercised to hinder God's plan or revelation, it is unjustified violence. Such illegitimate violence will only lead to further violence (Matt. 26:52).

14. Later during one of His trials, Jesus said He could call

upon an entire army of angels to fight for Him if He wished to be delivered from death (Matt. 26:53).

Obviously, Jesus felt that the use of such force in certain circumstances would be perfectly just. But Christ had come to fulfill the Old Testament prophecies concerning His death (Matt. 26:54). This explains why Jesus did not call upon His disciples or the angels of God to fight for Him. It was not because He was a pacifist, but because He had come to die for our sins.

In the light of these fourteen points, we can logically conclude that the most probable position of Jesus according to the Gospel data is that He supported the scriptural use of force in personal or civil defense. From the beginning to the end of His ministry, Jesus spoke with approval of the just use of force. At no time did He condemn it.

THE SERMON ON THE MOUNT

Of all the sermons which the Son of God preached to the multitudes, the Sermon on the Mount has always been the favorite of God's people. Even non-Christian scholars acknowledge the amazing depth, clarity, and practicality of this sermon. Its ethical force lives on in the hearts of people all over the world.

In order for us to understand this passage of Scripture in all of its depth and beauty, we must be careful to observe the principle of context. Christ is contrasting His view of the inner spirituality of the law of God to the externalized legalistic interpretation of the law that had arisen in rabbinic Judaism.

This is important to point out because a superficial reading of the sermon might lead some to think that Christ was attacking the Old Testament Scriptures. Indeed, some commentators interpret the Sermon on the Mount as the place where Jesus contrasted His New Testament ethic of love with the Old Testament ethic of hate. They claim Jesus directly rejected the Old Testament. Marcion felt this way, too. Marcionism was one of the ancient heresies condemned by the early church. It pitted the New Testament against the Old Testament.

Marcion taught that the Old Testament was worthless so far as a Christian was concerned.[1]

The early Christians condemned Marcion's position on the Old Testament for several reasons.

1. Christ began this sermon by assuring His audience that He had not come to destroy the Old Testament (Matt. 5:17). Indeed, this would have been impossible because the smallest stroke in the law must be fulfilled (v. 18). Furthermore, anyone who attacks the Old Testament, misinterprets its commands or encourages people to break its laws, will be least in the kingdom of heaven (v.19).

With Christ's disclaimer at the beginning of His sermon, it is impossible to interpret His subsequent words as an attack on the Old Testament Scriptures.

2. In Matt. 5:20, Jesus zeroes in on what He is going to deal with in His sermon when He refers to "the righteousness of the Pharisees." He refers to the traditions and teachings of rabbinic Judaism that had arisen during the intertestamental period. The Mishna, Midrash and Talmuds have preserved some of these traditions. (The intertestamental period is the time gap between the last book in the Old Testament and Jesus' birth, about 400 years.)

The Pharisees had become legalistic in their devotion to the traditional interpretation of the law as given by their fathers. They had voided the meaning of God's law through their man-made traditions. Thus Jesus and the Pharisees frequently fought over whether we should follow tradition or Scripture (see Mark 7:1–13 as an example).

3. Since Jesus was refuting the rabbinic interpretation of the law and not the law itself, He introduced His points by saying, "You have heard that it was said to people long ago . . . but I tell you . . ." (Matt. 5:21, 27, 33).

If He had been quoting Scripture, then He would have used His usual formula: "It is written. . . ." He was not rejecting the Old Testament, but the warped and twisted inter-

---

[1]John McClintock and James Strong, *Cyclopedia of Biblical, Theological, and Ecclesiastical Literature*, Vol. 5 (Grand Rapids: Baker Book House, 1981), p. 736.

pretation the Pharisees used when they explained it.

4. A final proof that Jesus was dealing with rabbinic law is found in verse 21 where He said, "Anyone who murders will be subject to judgment." This statement is not a quote from the Old Testament but from some rabbinical writing. Most modern commentators point this out clearly.[2]

Now that we have properly identified the context of the sermon, we can begin to make several observations on its content.

First, nowhere in this sermon does Jesus bring up the subject of the state or whether or not governments can protect their citizens with armed forces. He does not mention the subject of war at any point.

This is a vital point because the Sermon on the Mount has been incorrectly used at times to condemn all warfare. Jesus never brought up such subjects. So any claims that the Sermon on the Mount calls for national or international pacifism must be rejected as exegetically erroneous.

Second, Jesus is clearly discussing *personal ethics*. He is describing vital inner qualities of piety and the ways in which we should respond to our neighbors when they become sources of irritation.[3]

That is why Jesus could talk about loving one's neighbor, turning the other cheek and giving ones' coat to someone. At no point in the passage does Jesus discuss national or international ethics.

This last point is very important because it would be a basic logical error to assume that personal ethics can be applied to national or international situations without modification. It is rather simplistic to assume that the rules in Matthew 5 governing personal behavior during times of peace must be followed by nations in times of peace or war.

Third, while Jesus reestablishes the Old Testament principle that individuals should not seek personal vengeance (Lev.

---

[2]R. Lenski, *The Interpretation of St. Matthew's Gospel* (Minneapolis: Augsburg, 1933), p. 36.
[3]Carl Henry, *Christian Personal Ethics* (Grand Rapids: Baker Book House, 1977), pp. 306 ff.

19:18, Matt. 5:38–42), this can hardly be applied to the church or to the state. Both are under divine obligation to punish offenders.

The church has a moral obligation to punish an offending member even to the point of excommunication (Matt. 18:17; 1 Cor. 5:4, 5).

If personal ethics must apply to the church, then the church's use of moral, spiritual and ecclesiastical force in disciplining its members must be viewed as wrong. But if the church's use of spiritual force in disciplining its membership is correct, then the church has a unique set of rules to guide its behavior, not the personal ethics of Matthew 5.

The state has a moral obligation to punish offenders even to the point of death (Rom. 13:1–4). While it is wrong for individuals to take the law in their hands and punish people out of personal vengeance, the Scriptures clearly teach that the state is to use the sword to punish evildoers and to protect the good. The state cannot function on the basis of personal ethics if it is to fulfill its God-given task.

Fourth, Jesus was not discussing what to do if one's life is threatened or what to do if the life of a spouse or child is threatened. We are to avoid overreacting or exploding in anger when we receive personal insults. Don't be so quick to respond in like manner when evil is done to you. Don't be short-tempered but be patient and kind.

For example, in Matt. 5:39, Jesus specifically referred to the right cheek as being slapped instead of the left cheek because the slap of the right cheek by the back of the left hand was a personal insult and not an act of violence done in the context of war. Slapping the right cheek was not a life-threatening attack. It was a personal insult, like spitting in someone's face.[4]

Fifth, let us take a close look at some of Jesus' words which some people have mistakenly interpreted as teaching pacifism.

---

[4]Roland H. Bainton, *Christian Attitudes Toward War and Peace* (New York: Abingdon, 1960), p. 61.

"Blessed are the meek" (v. 5). We must not assume that meekness means weakness. This is clear from the simple observation that Moses was described as "very meek, more than any other man on the face of the earth" (Num. 12:3).

Since Moses was a man of strong, aggressive leadership and was involved in warfare, being "meek" has nothing to do with being passive toward evil or the enemies of God. The word itself carries the connotation of a quiet strength and resolution to overcome evil.

"Blessed are the peacemakers" (v. 9). The Greek word "peacemaker" was one of Caesar's titles.[5] He was called "the peacemaker" because he won and maintained peace by the use of force. The word does not mean "peaceable" or "pacifistic" or "peace at any price." The word meant "peace through strength." As such, it named the head of the Roman army without contradiction.

"Do not resist him that is evil" (v. 39). When Jesus gives us the general principle that we should not be quick in returning evil for evil, His subject is dealing with your neighbor. We should personally be willing to go the second mile in enduring personal insults in order to win our neighbors to Christ.

The idea that Jesus is here saying that no resistance of any kind is to be made against evil is absurd. Even extreme pacifists resist evil by peace demonstrations, hunger strikes, not paying taxes, denying the military draft. Yet nonviolent and passive resistance are still resistance.

Equally absurd is the idea that resistance against any kind of evil whatever is condemned by Jesus. The New Testament tells us to "resist the devil" (1 Pet. 5:9; James 4:7). Didn't Jesus resist the Pharisees (Matt. 23)? Aren't all Christians called upon to fight for the faith (Jude 3)? Are we not called upon to resist heretics (1 Tim. 1:3–11; Titus 1:9–11)? Certain kinds of evil should be endured while other kinds of evil must be resisted.

CONCLUSION

Our survey of the Gospels has revealed that Jesus supported the scriptural use of force for personal or national de-

---

[5]Ibid. p. 64.

fense. There is no evidence in the Gospel material that Jesus taught pacifism or nonresistance. On the other hand, Jesus' use of the just-war model as the basis for multiple parables and as the pattern for the Judgment Day revealed that He was not in any way uncomfortable with Old Testament teaching in this regard.

FOR REVIEW AND DISCUSSION

1. Did Jesus ever condemn the Old Testament's approval of the use of force?
2. How can we discover what Jesus might have said if He had been asked about Christians being involved in the military? Did He tell soldiers to desert their post?
3. Would Jesus use the just-war model as the basis of some of His parables if He and His hearers were pacifists? Would a modern pacifist bring up war and capital punishment without registering some kind of protest? Did Jesus ever register such protests when He brought up such things?
4. Did Jesus use force in cleansing the Temple, in escaping His enemies, or at His arrest?
5. Was Jesus rejecting the Old Testament in His "Sermon on the Mount"? Was He dealing with personal ethics or international justice? Can personal ethics be applied to the church and the state, or do they follow special rules?

3

The Apostles and the Epistles

The apostles sought to carry on the teaching of the law and the prophets as well as the teachings of Christ. For them, the gospel was just as much an Old Testament truth as it was a New Testament revelation (Rom. 1:1–3; 1 Cor. 15:3, 4). They looked to the Old Testament Scriptures for basic principles of doctrine and ethics.

The apostles were careful to point out when various aspects of the Old Testament ceremonial laws, for instance, were superseded by the finished work of Christ. The book of Hebrews is a prime example of this.

Therefore, it is significant that nowhere in the Acts or the Epistles do the apostles ever deal with such issues as whether or not the state can maintain a military force or a national police force. Why did the apostles never deal with such issues?

The Old Testament clearly taught that God leads armies and has established penal justice. Christ never disapproved of that position in the Gospels. If the apostles rejected the Old Testament position on war and now taught pacifism, this would have stirred as much controversy as the laying aside of circumcision.

The apostles assumed that the state had the right to use force to protect its citizens from enemies without and from criminals within who would be a danger. It was assumed that individuals as well as nations had the right to defend themselves. No controversy whatsoever surfaced over these issues.

If the apostles had condemned the Old Testament teaching on the use of force, they would have generated a great deal of controversy with the Jews. The enemies of the early church would not have left such a fruitful area of accusation and ridicule untouched. The silence of the New Testament in this regard, coupled with the silence of the Mishna and Talmud, clearly indicates that the apostolic church was not teaching pacifism in opposition to the teaching of the Old Testament.

When we survey the Epistles, we do not find a single place where the apostles exhorted Israel or Rome to disarm their military forces or where the apostles condemned war or a Christian's participation in the military. There is no indication that they taught anything different than what is found in the law.

THE ACTS

In the book of Acts, we have a record of the expansion of the early church. The church grew under a world power which maintained peace throughout the empire by its military presence.

This military presence enabled the early church to evangelize from city to city with safety. The early church expanded as a direct result of the military presence of the Roman empire.

In the book of Acts, not once is the military or political presence of Rome denounced. On the other hand, the Christians appealed to Rome for safety.

The following points from Acts lead us to the clear inference that the Apostles did not deny the use of force.

First, the apostles did not hesitate to use the force of civil disobedience when the government overstepped its authority. That is why Peter could say to his government leaders, "We must obey God rather than men" (Acts 5:29; 4:19).

The Scriptures view human authority in terms of delegated spheres of responsibilities. Each has specific duties and functions to carry out. Thus, all authority is delegated authority, and those who exercise authority will be accountable to God on Judgment Day.

The Scriptures speak of the spheres of the state, the church, and the family. These spheres are independent of each other, having separate functions and responsibilities. The leadership in a sphere has authority as long as it functions within the context of its divinely appointed tasks. Once they seek to dominate the other spheres or step out of the circle of their own responsibility, they no longer have any divinely delegated authority.

In this light, it is no wonder that Peter and the apostles felt the state had no authority to invade the church's sphere of authority and to determine who and what was to be preached. The moment the state stepped out of its own sphere of responsibility and tried to take authority from the church, it no longer had any delegated authority from God.

Whenever the state oversteps its delegated sphere of authority, it becomes tyranny. God has the ultimate authority over all spheres of authority, and He is to be obeyed rather than tyrants. This is why Peter could tell the tyrants of his day that he was not going to obey them.

Second, as the apostles evangelized Roman soldiers, they never told these new converts to leave the military. In Acts 10, Cornelius is set forth as an example of a respected soldier who remained in "the situation he was in when God called him" (1 Cor. 7:20). If the early church was pacifist, then there would be some indication that converts from the military were encouraged to desert their posts.

Third, when the Apostle Paul was opposed at the outset of his first missionary tour, he exercised divine force in causing a wicked magician to be blinded (Acts 13:6–11). Paul's missionary travels began with the use of force.

Fourth, when Paul was threatened by death, he did not hesitate to claim the political and military protection which was his as a Roman citizen (Acts 16:37–39; 22:25–29). If the early church believed that anyone involved with politics or the military was necessarily involved in evil, Paul would not have called upon either of them for protection.

Fifth, the Apostle Paul appealed for military protection from a death squad (Acts 23:12–27). If Paul was a pacifist and viewed all armed military force as sinful, he would not have called them for help. The fact that he did call them reveals that he did not view such force as intrinsically sinful.

Paul also appealed to Caesar to secure military protection from his enemies (Acts 25:11). The Apostle Paul would have been sent to Jerusalem had he not appealed to Caesar. Since he knew the Jews wanted to kill him, he appealed to Caesar to obtain armed military protection.

After he appealed to Caesar, the Apostle Paul was safe from assassination because of the presence of an armed guard. This protection allowed the Apostle freedom to write his prison epistles, to preach the gospel, and to win converts even in Caesar's household (Acts 28:16, 30, 31).

THE EPISTLES

The first mention of the state and its use of force to administer justice is found in Rom. 13:1–7. Paul is not dealing with the subject of war or whether or not Christians should be involved in war. However, it is clear from the passage that the state may use the sword, or force, to keep peace within society as the ministers of God. Rom. 13:1–7 is thus describing the internal police policies of punishing criminals and protecting citizens.

In this passage the Apostle Paul states that human government has been ordained of God to function in a certain way. A government that has been ordained of God uses force, the sword, to punish the wicked and to protect and reward the righteous. Thus God-ordained government is to be obeyed and respected because of its divinely appointed tasks. The Apostle states that we should pay taxes to such governments, for they are the servants of God, functioning according to God's law.

When a government abandons its delegated sphere of responsibility, overstepping its bounds and invading the sphere of the church or the family, it is no longer a divinely appointed government. It has become a tyrannical power. The word *tyrant* means someone who has usurped authority that does not belong to him. A government may be in power, but it is not necessarily the divinely appointed government.

A government is viewed as being tyrannical when it consistently punishes the righteous and protects and rewards the wicked, when it consistently invades other spheres and seeks to dominate all life by sheer force. Such a government is not ordained of God and should be resisted by the believer.

The second passage in the Epistles which deals with the state is found in 1 Tim. 2:1, 2. In this passage the Apostle Paul exhorts Christians to pray for their government leaders that these leaders will punish the wicked and protect the righteous, thus enabling believers to lead "tranquil and quiet lives." The Apostle's clear concern in his exhortation is that we should pray for our government that it will not overstep its authority and seek to tyrannize our lives.

The third passage is found in Heb. 11:32–40. The Old Testament saints who were "valiant in battle," "subdued kingdoms," and "put armies to flight" are set before Christian heroes of the faith to imitate. There is no hint here that the author of Hebrews felt the use of force in such contexts was somehow immoral or wrong. He has nothing but praise for such acts of courage. The freedom fighters of the Old Testament are set forth as examples of those whose faith enabled them to overcome evil in their own generation. Thus, Christians who follow in their train are to be praised and not condemned.

The last passage in the New Testament dealing specifically with the state is 1 Pet. 2:13–17. The Apostle Peter views the function of human government in exactly the same way that Paul did in Romans 13. Divinely ordained government is "to punish those who do wrong and to commend those who do right."

The Apostle Peter encourages believers to respect divinely appointed human government. He commands them to submit to its human institutions, such as the military draft, for the

Lord's sake. This clear passage speaks of the function of true government and how believers are to respond to its institution.

The above passages are the only ones in the Epistles which approach the issues with which we are concerned. It is rather obvious that the Epistles do not directly address themselves to the abstract issues of whether or not a nation can maintain military and police forces and whether or not a believer may be involved in military or political life. These things were not addressed because there was no controversy over them.

There is one last point that can be legitimately made. The authors of the New Testament used several military illustrations in describing the Christian life. They consistently viewed Christians as militant and not passive. As one surveys the New Testament, one cannot find a single instance where a passive model or nonresistant model is used to describe the Christian life. On the other hand, Christians are compared to active soldiers, farmers, and athletes. The apostles emphasize militant activism, not passive nonresistance.

The Christian life is viewed as a warfare against the forces of darkness (Eph. 6:10–19). Because of this warfare, the believer needs supernatural weapons (2 Cor. 10:3, 4). Every Christian is to view himself as a militant soldier for Jesus Christ (2 Tim. 2:3, 4). The church on earth is viewed as "the church militant" in that it is storming the gates of hell itself (Matt. 16:18).

The most we can logically deduce from the New Testament's use of the military motif in its descriptions of the Christian life is that the apostles were not uncomfortable with the idea of military life *per se*. If they were convinced that all connection with the military was intrinsically sinful and immoral, they would not have used the military as an illustration of the Christian life. A modern example would be the impossibility of using prostitution as a model for describing the Christian life.

CONCLUSION

Nowhere in the New Testament do the apostles directly or indirectly repudiate civil or personal defense. Nowhere in the

New Testament is the Christian in the army exhorted to resign from his post. Nowhere are believers forbidden to enter political or military life. The few passages in the Epistles which deal with human government speak of its divinely approved use of force to punish evildoers and to reward the righteous under God's blessing.

FOR REVIEW AND DISCUSSION

1. Did the Apostles ever condemn the Old Testament approval of the use of force? If they did this, would not the Jews have used this against them? Is there any record of the Jews attacking the Apostles on this point?
2. Did the Apostles give the state the "sword" to punish evil doers and to protect the innocent? Where in the New Testament can we find the answer?
3. Did the Apostles ask converts from the military to resign or desert their posts?
4. How did Paul avoid being killed by his enemies in Acts 23?
5. Did the Apostles disobey the state when it stepped out of its authority?

4

The Early Church and War

The early church's beliefs about war have become a source of heated debate. Pacifists have dogmatically stated that all the Christian leaders before Constantine rejected war as immoral and renounced the military as an occupation for any Christian. For example, Roland Bainton in *Christian Attitudes Toward War and Peace* stated, "All of the outstanding writers of the east and of the west repudiated participation in warfare for Christians."[1] This position has also been argued by Cadoux in *The Early Christian Attitude to War*.

On the other hand, Protestant church historians such as Philip Schaff, Harnack, McGiffert, Moffat, Lee, Frend, and archeologists such as Sir William Ramsey have also made a special study of the early church in this regard. They have come away convinced that the pacifists have overstated their case and ignored significant evidence that Christians were involved in the military from the apostolic period to Constantine.

Protestant historians have also noted that only two, or possibly three, Church Fathers were openly opposed to Christians participating in the military. Their grounds for rejecting military life is clearly the military's involvement with idolatry. The military required an oath and certain garments of cloth-

---

[1]Roland H. Bainton, *Christian Attitudes Toward War and Peace* (New York: Abingdon, 1960), p. 73.

ing, ceremonies and symbols which were idolatrous in nature.

Protestant historians such as Philip Schaff do not see any condemnation of war *per se* in the writings of the early Church Fathers. There is no indication that the Church Fathers rejected a nation's right to go to war to protect its citizens. Harnack argued this position in his *Militia Christi* in 1905. The argument has been brought up to date by John Helgeland in *Christians and the Roman Army, A.D. 173–337*.[2]

Roman Catholic scholars have traditionally taken a position exactly opposite the pacifists. While pacifists claim all the early writers as pacifists, the Catholics do not see any of the early writers as pacifists. This is most ably argued by Ryan in "The Rejection of Military Service by the Early Church."[3]

METHODOLOGY

Having surveyed the pacifist literature on the early church, it has become increasingly clear that the pacifists' methodology in their historical research and presentation rests on several faulty assumptions.

First, they assume that the apostolic period began with pure pacifism and that the church remained pure until Constantine. During Constantine's reign, the church "fell" from grace. The church suddenly abandoned its pacifism and pragmatically joined the military in order to support the first Christian emperor.

This argument includes several unwarranted assumptions and ignores some important facts. Since the New Testament never condemned war *per se* or the Christian's participation in the military, the Christian Church did not begin with pacifism. The New Testament carried on the Old Testament ethic of the just use of force for personal or civil defense. The apostolic age began with Christians such as Cornelius remaining in the army.

---

[2]John Helgeland, "Christians and the Roman Army A.D. 173–337," *Church History*, Vol. 43 (1974).

[3]E. Ryan, "The Rejection of Military Service by the Early Church," *Theological Studies*, Vol. 13 (March 1952).

For example, none of the earliest writers, such as Polycarp (A.D. 70–155), uttered one word against war or against Christians participating in the military. There is no evidence that the issue of war or the Christian's participation in the army ever occurred to the Church Fathers. They assumed that believers would remain in whatever calling or occupation they were employed in when converted.

Second, the supposed "fall" of the church from pacifism to approval of war with Constantine is a convenient myth which has no historical justification whatsoever. If the early church was committed to pacifism in principle, if they viewed war as intrinsically immoral and in conflict with Christ's teaching, to think that all of them would change their convictions simply because a Christian emperor came on the scene is quite unbelievable. We must remember that these are the same believers who went bravely to their deaths rather than deny what they believed. That they would change their pacifist beliefs and convictions for a Christian emperor is as plausible as believing that all modern-day pacifists will abandon their position once a Christian is elected President or Prime Minister. Just as modern pacifists would not change their conviction because of the arrival of Christian leadership, neither would the early pacifists have changed their convictions for the same reason.

The pacifists' assumption that the church "fell" with Constantine actually militates against their own position. They teach that the church changed its beliefs because there was a change of circumstances. Christians like Tertullian, who were outspoken in their rejection of Christians participating in the military, objected not because they were against war in principle or against Christians being in the military in principle, but because of the *idolatrous circumstances* connected with military life. As soon as Constantine changed those idolatrous circumstances, there no longer remained any reason why Christians should hesitate to be in the army.

The second methodological problem with the pacifist position is that they take statements out of context and then misapply them. For example, Polycarp applied the Old and

New Testament teaching against the use of violence for *personal* vengeance.[4] Some have seized upon this as proof that Polycarp was a pacifist. But nowhere in the context of the passage does Polycarp bring up the subject of war, Christians in the military, or whether the state has the right to maintain an army or a police force. General statements such as "do not render evil for evil, cursing for cursing," etc., should not be illegitimately applied to national defense when the author does not make the application himself. We must remember that in the Old Testament the prophets could preach against taking personal vengeance against one's enemies and, at the same time, encourage the nation of Israel to destroy the enemies of God. There is no inherent contradiction between denying personal vengeance and approving participation in just wars.

The third problem with the pacifists' methodology is that they try to prove more than the evidence they present can bear. For example, pacifists declare that governments should disarm and reject all warfare, even defensive wars. Therefore, they have to show that the early Christians believed that force was unjust *in principle* and that all governments should disarm and reject warfare.

When pacifists seek to prove their position, they frequently overstate their case, as they do with Origen. Origen did not want Christians to be in the military because of his spiritual and heavenly view of the Christian life. Yet he recorded this prayer of his for us:

> For those fighting in a righteous cause, and for the King who reigns righteously, that whatsoever is opposed to those who act righteously be destroyed.[5]

The same can be said of Tertullian. While it is clear that he did not want Christians to participate in the army because they would become defiled with idolatry, nowhere did Tertullian condemn the state for having an army. Neither did he condemn nations for going to war. He declared:

---

[4]Alexander Roberts and James Donaldson, editors, *Ante-Nicene Fathers* (Grand Rapids: Eerdmans Publishing Co., 1981), I:33.
[5]Ibid. IV:668.

> Without ceasing, for all our emperors, we offer prayer.
> We pray for life prolonged; for security to the empire; for
> protection to the imperial house; for *brave armies*. . . .[6]

If Origen or Tertullian were against the use of force *in principle* at any time, by anyone, including the state, they would hardly be found praying for those involved in righteous wars, that their soldiers would be brave in the destruction of their enemies.

When modern pacifists seek to prove their position by stating that the early church taught pure pacifism, they are overstating the case. Nowhere did the early Fathers teach that the use of force is intrinsically and morally wrong. The most the pacifists can come up with is an argument that some Christians did not believe they could, for conscience sake, because of idolatry, be involved in the military.

THE EVIDENCE

Church historians claiming that Christians were indeed involved in military life before Constantine have drawn their evidence from several different sources.

First, we have archeological evidence found on Christian tombstone inscriptions which identify the person buried as a Christian who was in the military. At least eight of these inscriptions are clearly pre-Constantine.[7]

If the church was totally pacifistic, condemning all participation in military life, it seems very unlikely that the relatives of a Christian would have gone to extra work to place his rank and legion on the tombstone. If being a soldier was a mark of shame and church discipline, we would not find a Christian's rank and the name of his legion on the tombstone.

Also, the physical presence of such Christian tombstones is undeniable evidence that Christians were involved in the army *before* Constantine. Sir William Ramsey, in his book *Luke the Physician*, comments on an inscription for a Christian soldier from Lycaonia. He argues that in A.D. 303, "it is certain

---

[6]Ibid. III:42.
[7]Diehl, *Inscriptiones Latinae Christanae* (Berlin, 1925–1931).

that the armies of the eastern empire were largely composed of Christians."[8]

The second line of evidence is found in the list of military martyrs prior to Constantine. In the very first church history, Eusebius recorded the history of many Christian soldiers who died for the faith.[9]

Eusebius's list of martyrs has been expanded by Musurillo in his book *The Acts of the Christian Martyrs*. While some of this material is clearly questionable, most of the martyrs in the military who died before Constantine have clear historical evidence behind them.

The third source of evidence is the history of the Christian Church in Armenia. Thaddeus, one of the seventy disciples whom Jesus sent out, was the first to preach the gospel in Armenia. Later the Apostle Bartholomew himself preached there.

Under the influence of Saint Gregory, Armenia became the first Christian nation in A.D. 303. When Maxminus tried to force the Armenians to renounce Christianity in A.D. 312, the Armenians took up arms and defended their faith and freedom. They defeated the Roman army.[10]

Throughout Armenian history, the Christian Church has never been pacifist. They have always defended their faith with the utmost courage and steadfastness.

The fourth source of evidence is the Thundering Legion (A.D. 173). Eusebius relates that soldiers in the Melitine Legion would kneel and pray before going into battle, as was the custom of Christians.[11] In a particular battle with Germans, the legion was in dire thirst. Due to the prayers of the Christian soldiers, God sent rain to refresh them while he sent lightning to confuse their enemies. The legion went on to triumph against their enemies due to the influence of the Christian soldiers.

---

[8]William Ramsey, *Luke the Physician and Other Studies in the History of Religion* (Grand Rapids: Baker Book House, 1979), pp. 339–395.

[9]*Eusebius's Ecclesiastical History* (Grand Rapids: Baker Book House, 1981), pp. 259, 283, 286, 317, 321–322, 347, 372, 389–390, 391–442, 435, 438.

[10]Ibid. p. 259.

[11]Ibid. p. 184.

Most pacifists simply ignore this incident or dismiss it as legendary. The defense of the historicity of the Thundering Legion has been stated by Phillip Schaff,[12] J. B. Lightfoot,[13] and by Frend.[14]

Since pagan Roman historians recount the same incident, it seems unlikely that Eusebius invented the story of the Thundering Legion.

The fifth line of argument comes from the apocryphal gospels. If the Christian Church was thoroughly pacifist in its view of Christ and the Christian life, why do we find so many accounts in the apocryphal gospels of Jesus using force to punish evildoers? For example, in *The Gospel of Thomas*,[15] Jesus is pictured as striking people dead.[16]

These stories are clearly fictitious; nevertheless, their presence in the popular literature of the early church reveals that believers did not view Jesus as a pacifist.

Or again, in the apocryphal *Acts of Paul*, written in A.D. 185, we read of Christian soldiers who were martyred for the faith while Paul was still living in Rome.[17] Christians living in A.D. 185 did not have any problems with believers being in the army. Such apocryphal works as *Acts of Paul* were widely read and enjoyed. This would never have happened if they were all pacifists.

Our last source of evidence is drawn from the theological writings of the early Church Fathers.

The pacifists have not been able to present one sentence from St. Clement (A.D. 30–100), Mathetes (A.D. 130), Polycarp (A.D. 155), Ignatius (A.D. 30–107), Papias (A.D. 70–155), Justin

---

[12]Phillip Schaff, *History of the Christian Church*, Vol. 2 (Grand Rapids: Eerdmans, 1973), p. 344.

[13]J.B. Lightfoot, *Apostolic Fathers*, part 2, Vol. 1 (Grand Rapids: Baker Book House, 1889, reprinted 1981), pp. 485–492.

[14]W. Frend, *Martyrdom and Persecution in the Early Church* (Grand Rapids: Baker Book House, 1965), p. 202, note 20.

[15]Edgar Hennecke, "The Gospel of Thomas," *New Testament Apocrypha*, Vol. 1, ed. Wilhelm Schneemelcher (Philadelphia: The Westminster Press, 1963), pp. 3, 4.

[16]Roberts, op. cit. VIII:395.

[17]Edgar Hennecke, "Acts of Paul," *New Testament Apocrypha*, Vol. 2, ed. Wilhelm Schneemelcher (Philadelphia: The Westminster Press, 1963), p. 384.

Martyr (A.D. 110–165), the epistles of Barnabus (A.D. 100), Ireneas (A.D. 120–202), the Shepherd of Hermas (A.D. 160), Tatian (A.D. 110–172), Athenagoras (A.D. 177), or Clement of Alexandria (A.D. 153–217), which in their respective contexts discuss whether war is justifiable or whether Christians can be involved in war.

The Fathers said many things dealing with personal ethics. When these statements are examined in their context, it is clear that the Father was not discussing war or the Christian's attitude toward the military. None of the above Fathers has anything to say about war *per se*.

When we study the early Fathers, we find they clearly taught that Christians could be found in all walks of life, including the military life.

Clement of Alexandria wrote:

> Practice husbandry, we say, if you are a husbandman; but while you till the fields, know God. Sail the sea, you who are devoted to navigation, yet call the whilst on the heavenly pilot. Has (saving) knowledge taken hold of you while engaged in military service? Listen to the commander who orders what is right. (II:200)[18]

If early Christians were pacifists, they surely would have stuck out in a society which used force. But the early Christian Fathers boasted that believers were not different in any way from their neighbors. In the Mathetes' letter to Diognetus, we find:

> Christians are distinguished from other men neither by country, nor language, nor the customs which they observe. For they neither inhabit cities of their own, nor employ a peculiar form of speech, nor lead a life which is marked out by any singularity . . . inhabiting Greek as well as Barbarian cities, according as the lot of each of them has been determined and following the customs of the nations in respect of clothing, food, and the rest of their ordinary conduct. (I:26)

Since Clement assumed that Christians were in the army

---

[18]All the following quotes in this chapter are from *The Ante-Nicene Fathers*, ed. Alexander Roberts and James Donaldson (Grand Rapids: Eerdmans, 1981). Only page numbers will be referred to.

when he dealt with the Christian's attitude toward various articles of clothing such as shoes, he commented:

> For a man bare feet are quite in keeping, except when he is on military service. (II:267)

Before he became a heretic, Tertullian argued that Christians functioned in every level of Roman society, including the military:

> We sail with you and fight with you, and till the ground with you; and in like manner we unite with you in your traffickings. (III:49)

When he was orthodox, Tertullian could pray for the armies of Rome to be brave in their protection of the empire (III:42).

Since the earliest Fathers never condemned Christians for being in the military, and they never rebuked the state for maintaining an army or a police force, the early church never condemned the use of force *per se*. It is no wonder that we cannot find a single instance in the early church where a Christian was refused membership or communion because he was a soldier. Nowhere do we find the teaching that Christians should desert their post.

Some view Tertullian's and Origen's writings as strong evidence of pacifism in the early church. Let's take a closer look at these two men and what they wrote.

TERTULLIAN (A.D. 160–215)

At the beginning of his ministry, Tertullian was quite orthodox in his theology. During this time he accepted the need for armies to fight righteous wars and recognized the presence of Christians in those armies (III:42, 49). After Tertullian joined the Montanist heretical movement with its ascetic view of life, Tertullian came to regard any contact with Rome as compromise with idolatry. The secular/sacred dichotomy can be found throughout Tertullian's later works.

Fourteen years after writing the apology where he approves of Christians participating in all of life, including the military, Tertullian wrote *De Corona Militis.*

In *De Corona Militis,* Tertullian exhorted Christians to withdraw from political and military life because the clothing, wreaths, oaths, and symbols of office had their origin in idolatry. Christians were expected to withdraw from all "secular" occupations and to give themselves to spiritual works (III:93–101).

In his book on idolatry (III:73), Tertullian explains why he felt that a Christian could not be involved with Rome at any point. He preached that a Christian could not hold any public office whatsoever. It did not matter if he were the mayor of a small village or a soldier in the army. Any association with Rome was an association with Satan himself. Not once in this work or any other work does Tertullian state that war *per se* is evil or that governments do not have the right to maintain armies and to exercise force to protect its citizens. He is not attacking soldiers specifically. He is bitterly denouncing Christians who were involved with Rome at any point. Tertullian withdrew to a secluded monastery in Egypt and established one of the first pacifist communities.

ORIGEN (A.D. 185–254)

Origen represented the earliest attempt to create a blend between Christianity and pagan philosophy. His many unorthodox views, such as the preexistence of the soul, led to his subsequent condemnation as a heretic by church councils.

In his reply to Celsus' demand that Christians should fight for the emperor regardless of what idolatry may be involved, Origen answered that Christians do in fact fight for the emperor but on a heavenly and spiritual plane (IV:667, 668).

While Christians could pray and fight spiritually for the empire,

> To those enemies of our faith who require us to bear arms
> for the Commonwealth, and to slay men, we cannot. (IV:668)

Origen believed that Christians were on a spiritual plane and should not become involved in such secular activities as war. He believed, nevertheless, that some wars were perfectly just and that it was the duty of Christians to pray that enemies of righteousness would be destroyed in such a war (IV:268). It is clear from his statements, that Origen was not a pacifist *in principle* because he did not believe that the use of force *per se* was evil.

As to Hippolytus, who said that Christians should not bear arms (V:256, Canon 14; 257, Canon 14), he did not explain why Christians should avoid military service. When he picks up the subject in his apostolic tradition (16;10–22), he deals with it in the context of idolatry and immorality. We are not explicitly told why he felt Christians should not be involved in the military.

Cyprian made one reference that has been seized upon as proof he was a pacifist. He stated:

> The hand spotted with the sword and blood should not receive communion. (V:488)

When we turn to the context for his statement concerning hands spotted with blood, we find that he was dealing with "adultery, fraud, and manslaughter." He was discussing *murder*, not military service *per se*, or killing someone in self-defense or in a war situation.

The Councils of Arles (A.D. 314) and Nice (A.D. 325) not only produced some of the great creeds of the church such as the Nicean Creed, but they both upheld the Christian's right to be involved in the military. They saw no controversy with believers being soldiers except when this necessarily involved idolatrous oaths or ceremonies.

St. Basil stated in A.D. 370:

> Our fathers did not think that killing in war was murder. (XIV:605)

While he did not see any biblical reason or apostolic tradition for cautioning taking communion after killing in a war situation, he went on to say that perhaps it would be good for a short period to avoid communion after killing in war.

CONCLUSION

We have surveyed the archeological and literary evidence concerning whether Christians participated in the military before Constantine, whether or not they condemned war in principle and the state's use of force in particular. The evidence demonstrates that Christians entered all areas of life from the beginning of the New Testament period. They did this because they viewed all areas of life as under the lordship of Christ. Christians could be found in every honorable profession from the military to that of sailors or farmers.

Only after the pagan philosophic idea of dividing life into a secular and sacred dichotomy invaded the Christian Church did we find a few writers who exhorted Christians to abandon all "secular" occupations. They felt Christians should avoid political and military life because of possible association with idolatrous practices.

Did any early Church Fathers set forth that it is *intrinsically* wrong for nations to use force to protect its citizens? When we turn to the evidence to see if any took this position, we find nothing. Not once is Rome called upon to disarm. Not once did Church Fathers urge nonresistance as a national policy.

Because of the idolatrous elements in the Roman army, some early Christians had a great struggle serving in the military. But once Constantine removed those idolatrous elements from military life, we do not find any other problems for Christians who desired to enter political or military professions.

FOR REVIEW AND DISCUSSION

1. What positions are taken by Roman Catholic, Protestant and Pacifist scholars as to whether the Early Church was pacifist?
2. What initial mistakes do most pacifist scholars make as they try to prove their position regarding the Early Church?
3. What evidence is there that the Apostolic and Early Fathers condemned the use of force by the state to punish criminals and to protect the nation?
4. What evidence does archeology provide regarding the Early Church's view of military service?

5. What significance do you give to the "Thundering Legion"? Do you think that such ancient churches as the Armenian Church would have used force if they had been taught pacifism at the beginning?

5

The Fathers and the Reformers

Down through the centuries the Christian Church has consistently recognized that civil governments have the biblical responsibility to protect the righteous and to punish the wicked. The state has a moral obligation to provide police protection and military defense. Criminal individuals or nations are to be punished with God's sword.

Christians are to view all of life as under Christ's lordship. They can participate in military and political careers. They can be policemen and soldiers as well as congressmen or presidents. Every square inch of life is to be claimed for Christ.

It is the duty of Christians to resist tyranny because tyranny seeks to take Christ's place as the Lord of all of life. This resistance can be either passive or active, depending on the situation. No private individual has the right to commit violence out of personal vengeance. But when oppressed people desire to depose a tyrant and political recourse is closed to them, force may be used.

Does this mean that Christians can be actively involved in overthrowing tyrannical powers? Our Fathers believed that if we take the many scriptural examples of such action seriously, all wars or revolutions fought to gain freedom from tyranny are just.

When is a government tyrannical? We should not judge a

government as tyrannical because of isolated acts of tyranny. A father may act tyrannically at times. Yet this does not give his children the right to take away his authority.

When a government tries to take control of *all* of life, it is tyrannical. The moment a government takes away the freedoms of religion, free speech, lawful assembly, etc., it is a tyrannical power and can be resisted.

The following readings are selections from the writings of the Church Fathers and the Reformers. It is no surprise to find that the clearest thinkers in the Christian Church have almost always believed in the just use of force.

Let the reader particularly note the writings of Goodman, Milton, and Rutherford, whose position on the right of revolution provided the theological basis of the American Revolution.

The churches in America were the driving force behind the American Revolution because of their Puritan theology of resistance to tyranny. They felt that they had a divine mandate to resist tyranny with their lives if necessary. The liberty we enjoy today in the Free World is due to their sacrifice.

Because some of the older English works are very rare and have not been reproduced for centuries, we have not edited the text or modernized the spelling. We have chosen this method in order to give scholars access to the original material.

ST. AUGUSTINE (A.D. 354–430)

Augustine was the greatest of the early Christian theologians. His writings dominated theological discussions during the Middle Ages and served as a basis of the Protestant Reformation. He saw clearly that war and peace are not irreconcilable opposites but that war can be the means of peace.

> The purpose even of war is peace. For, when victory is not followed by resistance there is a peace that was impossible so long as rivals were competing, hungrily and unhappily, for something material too little to suffice for both. This kind of peace is a product of the work of war, and its praise is a

so-called glorious victory; when victory goes to the side that had a juster cause it is surely a matter for human rejoicing.[1]

MANEGOLD OF LAUTENBACH (11th Century)

This scholastic theologian was fearless in defending the church's right to govern its own affairs without state interference. He taught that tyrannical powers can be abolished by the people because governments exist at the will of and for the good of the people. This idea later surfaced in the Scottish and American Revolutions where key documents begin by saying, "We the people . . ."

> if a king forsakes rule by law and becomes a tyrant, he is to be considered to have broken the pact [with the people] to which he owes his power and may be deposed by the people.[2]

THOMAS AQUINAS (1224–1274, A.D.)

Aquinas is viewed as the greatest theologian of the Roman Catholic Church and is still the official philosopher of that church.

> There are three conditions of a just war. First, the authority of the sovereign by whose command the war is to be waged. For it is not the business of the private individual to declare war or to summon the nation. The second condition is that hostilities should begin because of some crime on the part of the enemy. Wherefore Augustine observes that a just war is wont to be described as one that avenges wrongs, when a nation or state has to be punished for refusing to make amends for the injuries done by its people or to restore what has been seized unjustly. The third condition is a rightful intention, the advancement of good or the avoidance of evil. It may happen that a war declared by legitimate authority for a just cause may yet be rendered unlawful through a wicked intention. Hence Augustine declares that the passion of inflicting harm, the cruel thirst for vengeance, a plundering

---

[1]Augustine, *City of God Against the Pagans* (Cambridge: Harvard University Press), XV, ch. 4.
[2]Liber ad Gebehar dum, 47.

and implacable spirit, the fever of turmoil, the lust of power and suchlike, all these are justly condemned in war.[3]

FRANSIS SUAREZ (1548–1617, A.D.)

Suarez is referred to as the "father of international law" because he was the first to develop a systematic approach to international affairs. His writings guided European countries for centuries.

Is Sedition Intrinsically Evil?

1. Sedition is the term used to designate general warfare carried on within a single state, and waged either between two parts thereof or between the prince and the state. I hold, first, that sedition involving two factions of the state is always an evil on the part of the aggressor, but just on the defensive side. The truth of the latter statement is self-evident. The truth of the former is proved by the fact that no legitimate authority to declare war is discernible in such a situation, for this authority, as we have seen (Section II supra, p. 806), resides in the sovereign prince. The objection will be made that, sometimes, a prince will be able to delegate this authority, if urgent public necessity demands that he do so. In such a case, however, the prince himself, and not a part of the state, is held to be the aggressor; so that no sedition will exist in the sense in which we are using the term. But what if one part of the state actually suffers injury from another part, and is unable to secure its right through the prince? My reply is that this injured part may do nothing beyond that which a private individual may do, as can easily be gathered from what we have said above.

2. I hold, secondly, that a war of the state against the prince, even if it be aggressive, is not intrinsically evil; but that the conditions necessary for a war that is in other respects just must nevertheless be present in order that this sort of war may be righteous. This conclusion holds true only when the prince is a tyrant, a situation which may occur in one of two ways, as Cajetan notes (on II.–II, qu. 64, art. 1, ad 3 [art. 3]). In the first place, the prince may be a tyrant in regard to his [assertion of tyrannical] dominion, and power; secondly,

---

[3]Thomas Aquinas, *Summa Theologica*, Vol. 35 (New York: McGraw-Hill Book Co., 1964), 2a–2ac.xl.l.

he may be so merely in regard to his acts of government.

When the first kind of tyranny occurs, the whole state, or any portion thereof, has the right [to revolt] against the prince. Hence, it follows that any person whatsoever may avenge himself and the state against [such] tyranny. The reason supporting these statements is that the tyrant in question is an aggressor, and is waging war unjustly against the state and its separate parts, so that, in consequence, all those parts have the right of defence. Such is the opinion expressed by Cajetan (loc. cit.); and this conclusion may also be derived from a passage in St. Thomas's works (on the *Sentences*, Bk. II, dist. xliv, qu. 2, art. 2).

John Huss upheld the same doctrine with respect to the second kind of tyrant, and, indeed, with respect to every unjust superior . . .

The proof of these assertions is as follows: the prince in question is, we assume, the true sovereign; and inferiors have not the right of declaring war, but only that of defending themselves, a right which does not apply in connexion with this sort of tyrant; for the latter does not always do wrong to individuals, and in any attack which [these individuals] might make, they would be obliged to confine themselves to necessary self-defence. The state as a whole, however, may rise in revolt against such a tyrant; and this uprising would not be a case of sedition in the strict sense, since the word is commonly employed with a connotation of evil. The reason for this distinction is that under the circumstances described the state, as a whole, is superior to the king, for the state, when it granted him his power, is held to have granted it upon these conditions: that he should govern in accord with the public weal, and not tyrannically; and that, if he did not govern thus, he might be deposed from that position of power.

[In order that such rebellion may justly occur,] however, the situation must be one in which it is observed that the king does really and manifestly behave in a tyrannical manner; and the other conditions laid down for a just war must concurrently be present. On this point, see St. Thomas (*De Regimine Principum*, Bk. I, chap. vi).[4]

MARTIN LUTHER (1483–1546, A.D.)

Luther was no doubt the "father" of the Protestant Reformation. His reliance on the Scriptures alone and his bold

---

[4]*Selections From Three Works of Fransis Suarez*, Classics of International Law, No. 20, vol. II, pp. 854–855.

message of justification by faith alone changed the course of Western civilization forever.

> A prince and a lord must remember that according to Romans 13[:4] he is God's minister and the servant of his wrath and that the sword has been given to him to use against such [wicked] people. If he does not fulfill the duties of his office by punishing some and protecting others, he commits as great a sin before God as when someone who has not been given the sword commits murders. If he is able to punish and does not do it—even though he would have had to kill someone or shed blood—he becomes guilty of all murder and evil that these people commit.[5] (*Against the Robbing and Murdering Hordes*, [1522])

In the passage above Luther was pleading for the civil authorities to stop the Radical Anabaptists who had gone on a rampage of murder, rape and looting during the Peasant's War. This war caused the deaths of over 100,000 people. Some of these Anabaptists were committed to the practice of common property and common marriage. They have been called "The first communists."[6]

JOHN CALVIN (1509–1564)

While Luther was the founder of the Reformation, Calvin was its most popular systematic theologian. His theology helped form the basis of the political freedoms which the West now enjoys.

> Then let God be feared in the first place, and earthly princes will obtain their authority, if only God shines forth, as I have already said. Daniel, therefore, here defends himself with justice, since he had not committed any crime against the king; for he was compelled to obey the command of God, and he neglected what the king had ordered in opposition to it. For earthly princes lay aside all their power when they rise up against God, and are unworthy of being reckoned in the number of mankind. We ought rather utterly to defy than to obey them when they are so restive and wish to spoil God of

---

[5] *Against the Robbing and Murdering Hordes*, 1522.
[6] Norman Cohn, *The Pursuit of the Millennium* (New York: Oxford University Press, 1970), pp. 250–280.

his rights, and as it were, to seize upon his throne and draw him down from heaven.[7]

I am speaking all the while of private individuals. For if there are now any magistrates of the people, appointed to restrain the willfulness of kings (as in ancient times the ephors were set against the Spartan kings, or the tribunes of the people against the Roman consuls, or the demarchs against the senate of the Athenians; and perhaps, as things now are, such power as the three estates exercise in every realm when they hold their chief assemblies), I am so far from forbidding them to withstand, in accordance with their duty, the fierce licentiousness of kings, that, if they wink at kings who violently fall upon and assault the lowly common folk, I declare that their dissimulation involved nefarious perfidy, because they dishonestly betray the freedom of the people, of which they know that they have been appointed protectors by God's ordinance.[8]

ZWINGLI (1489–1531, A.D.)

Zwingli was the leader of the Swiss Reformation and was known as the "fighting priest" because he died in battle defending his family, church and nation. As a pastor with a true shepherd's heart, he fought to protect his sheep from the wolves though it cost him his life.

Many clergymen followed his example of courage and self-sacrifice by taking up arms during the Scottish and American Revolutions.

EXPOSITION OF THE CHRISTIAN FAITH

CHAPTER VII

GOVERNMENTS

The Greeks recognize these three kinds of governments with their three degenerate forms: monarchy, which the Latins call "regnum, kingdom," where one man stands alone as the head of the state under the guidance of piety and justice. The opposite and degenerate form is a tyranny, which the

---

[7]John Calvin, *Commentary* on Daniel 6:22.
[8]John Calvin, *Institutes of the Christian Religion* (Philadelphia: Westminster Press, 1967), IV. XX:31.

Latins less fittingly call "vis" or "violentia," "force," or "violence," or rather, not having quite the proper word themselves, they generally use "tyrannis," borrowing the word from the Greeks. This exists when piety is scorned, justice is trodden under foot, and all things are done by force, while the ruler holds that anything he pleases is lawful for him. Secondly, they recognize an aristocracy, which the Latins call "optimatium potentia, the power of the best people," where the best men are at the head of things, observing justice and piety towards the people. When this form degenerates it passes into an oligarchy, which the Latins call literally "paucorum potentia, the power of the few." Here a few of the nobles rise up and gain influence who, caring not for the general good but for private advantage, trample upon the public weal and serve their own ends. Finally they recognize a democracy, which the Latins render by "res publica, republic," a word of broader meaning than democracy, where affairs, that is, the supreme power, are in the hands of the people in general, the entire people; and all the civil offices, honors, and public functions are in the hands of the whole people. When this form degenerates, the Greeks call it "sustremma a sustasis" that is, a state of sedition, conspiracy, and disturbance, where no man suffers himself to be held in check, and instead each one, asserting that he is a part and a member of the people, claims the power of the state as his own, and each one follows his own reckless desires. Hence there arise unrestrained conspiracies and factions, followed by bloodshed, plundering, injustice and all the other evils of treason and sedition.

These distinct forms of government of the Greeks I recognize with the following corrections: If a king or prince rules, I teach that he is to be honored and obeyed, according to Christ's command, "Render unto Caesar the things that are Caesar's and unto God the things that are God's" [Luke 20:25]. For by "Caesar" I understand every ruler upon whom power has been conferred or bestowed, either by hereditary right and custom or by election. But if the king or prince becomes a tyrant, I correct his recklessness and inveigh against it in season and out of season. For thus saith the Lord to Jeremiah, "See, I have . . . set thee over the nations and over the kingdoms," etc. [Jer. 1:10]. If he listens to the warning, I have gained a father for the whole kingdom and fatherland, but if he becomes more rebelliously violent, I teach that even a wicked ruler is to be obeyed until the Lord shall remove him from his office and power or a means be found to enable those whose duty it is to deprive him of his functions and restore order.[9]

ON TRUE AND FALSE RELIGION

Second, they are wrong in not understanding that Christ is speaking here of a tyranny rather than of a monarchy or an aristocracy conferred by consent of the people or by the calling of God upon one to whom the office of preaching the Word has not been committed. I call it tyranny when dominion is assumed on one's own authority. If one man does this, he is a tyrant, and his sway is called a tyranny; if several, not all but some few, arrogate dominion to themselves, the Greeks called it an oligarchy. Tyranny, then, Christ altogether forbids. . . . "It frequently happens on this wise that when we raise even a pious man to a position of authority he degenerates into an impious one." Why do you complain of that? You have thus just what you want—an impious ruler set over you. But away with quibbling! If, then, a pious ruler degenerates into an impious one, remove this impious one and substitute a pious one. . . . Swords are carried before certain rulers as an emblem of power, and it is to this custom that Paul is alluding here. He shows that some are so audaciously evil that, unless they be smitten with the sword, the rest cannot have peace. He says, therefore, that the ruler is a minister of God for the guarding of general righteousness and tranquillity. Here I ask those who repudiate the magistracy whether a pious man cannot be a minister of Christ just as well as an impious man. They say it was written among them of old time [cf. Mt. 5:21f.]: "Thou shalt not kill"; but that we are forbidden to yield to anger, much more to kill. Nice fellows these! They refuse with the very words before them to see what the meaning of God's words is. For when He says that we are not even to yield to anger, it becomes clear that, wishing to block up the fountain-source of killing, He is speaking of that killing which proceeds from ungovernable passion, not of that which is visited by law upon those who have dared to upset the public peace, towards whom we more often feel pity than anger. But, since even in such cases judgment is sometimes too precipitate, is not a pious man more likely to give a right and timely judgment than an impious man?—"For he is a minister of God, an avenger for wrath to him that doeth evil" (Rom. 13:4). He says he is a minister of

---

[9]*Works of Zwingli*, Vol. II, pp. 161, 162.

God and an avenger whom He uses for wrath, that is, to assert His justice, against those who do evil. He, therefore, avenges in God's name, not in his own: He smites in God's name.[10]

BULLINGER (1504–1575, A.D.)

Bullinger was the next leader of the Swiss reformation after Zwingli was killed. Some of his theological writings are still being published to this day because of their depth of learning.

For the apostles according to their manner fight as apostles, not with the spear and sword and bow of physical warfare, but of spiritual. The apostolic sword is the Word of God. (26) Meanwhile no one denies that the weapons of physical or corporal warfare have from time to time been of advantage to apostolic men and the Church, and do good even today. (27) No one denies that God does frequently use the help of soldiers and magistrates in defending the Church against the wicked and tyrants: on the contrary, everyone will confess that the good and godly magistrate has his duty to the Church of God. For not without great cause does the worthy prophet of God, Isaiah, call "kings nursing fathers and queens nursing mothers." Paul, when he is oppressed by the Jews in the temple at Jerusalem for preaching the Gospel among the Gentiles, is taken away and rescued by the army of Claudius Lysias, the tribune. And not long after the same tribune sent with the apostle no small company of soldiers, that is, a troop of horsemen and certain companies of footmen, by whom he was brought safely to Antipatris and Caesarea before Felix the proconsul of Judea; as Luke recalled, not hastily, but with much diligence and in great detail in the Acts of the Apostles. Ecclesiastical history recites many instances of holy princes who have defended and succoured the Church of God.[11]

JOHN WOLLEBIUS (1586–1629, A.D.)

Wollebius is considered by many the greatest theologian during the early seventeenth century. His works were translated and studied throughout Europe.

---

[10]Works of Zwingli, Vol. III, pp. 298, 301, 313.
[11]*Zwingli and Bullinger*, Library of Christian Classics, Vol. 24, ed. G.W. Bromiley, (Philadelphia: Westminster Press, 1979), p. 314.

PROPOSITIONS

I. It is permissible for Christians to wage war, no less than it was formerly for the Jews.

The reason is that it is not forbidden anywhere in the New Testament, and also that the centurion at Capernaeum (Mt. 8:5–13), and Cornelius the Centurion (Acts 10) are included among the believers. What John urged soldiers to give up was not war, but injustice (Lk. 3:14).

II. War must be waged, not by private authority, but by that of the magistrate.

III. War must not be waged unless it is just and necessary.

IV. A war will be just with respect to matter, form, and purpose if it is waged in a just case, for a good purpose, and according to the commandment of the word of God.

V. A war will be necessary, if an effort has first been made to settle the dispute by peaceful means rather than by arms.

VI. Once war has begun, it does not matter whether it is carried on by force or by ambush and craftiness.

VII. Deceit that is combined with lying (mendacio) and the breaking of treaties cannot be approved, but if it is accomplished (merely) by concealing the truth (dissimulation) it may be approved.

VIII. Although the church is established by the Word, not by the sword, yet, once it has been established, it may justly be defended by arms against unjust force.[12]

GEORGE BUCHANAN (1506–1582)

Buchanan was one of the great lights of the Scottish reformation. He vigorously refuted the doctrine of the "divine right of kings," which was used by rulers in those days to justify their most wicked deeds. This led him eventually to the idea of a democratic state where the people could choose their own leaders.

The following are quotes from DE JURE REGNI APUD SCOTOS (1579):

> The people, from whom (the King) derived his power, should have the liberty of prescribing (limiting) its bounds: I require that (the King) should exercise over the people only those rights which he has received from their hands. (p. 262)

---

[12]*Reformed Dogmatics*, ed. Beardslee, III (New York: Oxford University Press, 1965), pp. 327–328.

(They were) tyrants . . . because they were superior to the laws. (p. 260)

A king rules over a willing (people), a tyrant over a reluctant people. . . . Tyranny (is) a master's (power) over his slaves. . . . Tyrants (rule) for the oppression of [their] citizens. (p. 261)

If (the King) extorted obedience from the people by force, the people . . . may shake off so grievous a yoke . . . every system upheld by violence may, by the like violence, be overturned. (p. 264)

SAMUEL RUTHERFORD (1600–1661)

Rutherford is aptly described as being the father of both the Scottish and American Revolutions. We must never forget the major role that Americans of Scottish descent played in the American revolution. Rutherford and the other Scottish reformers gave Americans the theoretical justification for their revolution and the ideas later written in the Constitution.

The following are quotes from LEX REX (1644):

Tyranny being a work of Satan is not from God, because sin, whether habitual or actual, is not from God. . . . A power ethical, politic, or moral to oppress (people) is not of God, and is not a (valid) power; and is no more from God, but from sinful nature and the old serpent, than a license to sin. (p.32)

We teach that any priest may kill a tyrant, void of all title. . . . If (the tyrant) have not the consent of the people, he is a usurper, for we know of no external (autonomous) calling that kings have now, or their family, to the crown, but only the call of the people. (p. 38)

God hath given no absolute and unlimited power to a king above the Law. (p. 101)

Absolute power to tyrannise over the people and to destroy them is not a power from God. (p. 102)

It is lawful for the subjects in any use to take arms against the lawful king, if he degenerated and shall wickedly use his lawful power. (p. 134)

If a king should sell his kingdom, and invite a bloody conqueror to come in with an army of men to destroy his people; impose upon their conscience an idolatrous religion, they may lawfully rise against that army without the King's consent. . . . The king's power of wars is for the safety of his people, if he deny his consent to the raising of arms till they be destroyed he playeth the tyrant, not the King. (p. 18)

JOHN LILBURNE (1618–1657)

Lilburne's fearless opposition to tyranny earned this Quaker preacher the title "Freedom John." The following quote is from his work, LEGITIMATE DEFENSE (1653):

> The Most authentic servants of Christ have always been the worse enemies of tyranny and the oppressor.

A HIND LET LOOSE (1680)

The exact author of this work is not known. Some think that it was written by Buchanan. It was written at a time when if it were known whom the author was, he would have been put to death. This work was extremely popular in its day because it boldly dealt with the issue of

> Whether a people, long oppressed with the encroachments of tyrants and usurpers, may disown their pretended authority. (p. 275)

What is a "tyrant"? (The) characters of a tyrant are:

> 1. He that doth not receive a government by the will of the people, but by force invadeth it, or intercepteth it by fraud, is a tyrant; and who dominates even over the unwilling (for rex volentibus tyrannus invitis imperat) and provides the Supreme rule without the people's consent, even though for several years they may so govern. . . .
> 2. He does not govern for the subject's well-fare or publick utility but for himself. . . .
> 3. Tyranny is against nature and a masterly principality over slaves. . . . When he begins to invade his subjects rights and liberties . . . he loses all legal power in and over an army or Empire, who by that government and army does obstruct the welfare of that republick. . . .
> 4. A tyrant is he, who takes away from one or more members of the common wealth the free exercise of the orthodox religion. (pp. 283–289)
> Being quite out wearied by a continual tract of Tyrannical oppression, arbitrarily enacted by wicked laws, and illegally executed against their own laws, and cruelly prosecuted even without all color of law, in many unheard of barbarities when there could be no access for a success in complaining or getting redress by law, all petitions and remonstrance of grievances being declared sedition and treasonable, and inter-

preted as such; they were forced to betake themselves to this remedy of defense resistance, intending only the preservation of their lives, religion, and liberties. (p. 577)

It is lawful to rebell against Tyrants. (p. 580)

We are not for rising in arms for triffles of our own things, or small injuries done to our selves, but in a case of necessity for the preservation of our lives, religion, laws and liberties, when all that are dear to us as men and Christians are in hazard: So we are not for rising up in arms to force the magistrate to be of our religion, but to defend our religion against his force. (p. 587)

BRUTUS (?–1689)

Brutus was another of the Scottish reformers who was devoted to freedom. The following quotes are from his work A DEFENSE OF LIBERTY AGAINST TYRANTS:

Whether subjects are bound and ought to obey princes if they command that which is against the Law of God . . . God must rather be obeyed than man. (p. 65)

Is it lawful to resist a prince violating the Law of God, or ruinating the Church, or hindering the restoring of? If we hold ourselves to the tendure of the Holy Scriptures it will resolve us for. . . . It had been lawful to the Jewish people (to rebell against tyranny). . . . The same must be allowed to the whole people of any Christian Kingdom or country whatsoever. (p. 87)

Justice requires that tyrants and destroyers of the commonwealth be compelled to reason. Charity (demands) the right of relieving and restoring the oppressed. Those who make no account of these things, do as much as in their lies to drive piety, justice, and charity out of this world that they may never more be heard of. (p. 229)

THOMAS MANTON (1620–1677)

One of the most loved English Puritans of the seventeenth century, Manton's complete works are still being published and studied today. Manton preached in difficult times when a tyrannical king had reached the point where he made it a crime punishable by death or imprisonment to preach anything that he did not like.

There is nothing in Scripture expressly against (just wars), nothing but strained consequences, as that of Matt.V.43,44, concerning love of enemies, which is forced; for nothing is there commanded but what is commanded in the Old Testament. Now these (O.T.) wars are approved, yea, appointed by God; and that saying of Christ concerneth private persons forbidding private revenge, passions, and animosities; and so likewise Matt.V.39, where we are forbidden to resist, must be understood of the retaliation of private revenge; and so that of Rom.XII.19–21, "Avenge not yourselves." The magistrate's vengeance is God's vengeance; he is a person authorized by the Lord; therefore is it forbidden to a private person–he is not God's minister–to avenge them that do ill, and etc.[13]

CHRISTOPHER GOODMAN (1520–1602)

Goodman's stand against the tyrannical reign of the infamous queen, rightly remembered as "Bloody Mary," forced him into exile in fear of his life. While he could not speak to his fellow citizens in person, his books were widely read even though the punishment for such a "crime" was death! Goodman's title for this work feels laboriously long to us, but was not unusual for his time: *How Superior Powers ought to be obeyd of their subjects: and Wherin they may lawfully by Gods Worde be disobeyed and resisted. Wherin also is declared the cause of all this present miserie in England, and the only way to remedy the same.*

The following quotes are from this work:

Whence hath (the King) this honor? Of himself? Is any man naturally born a King, or hath he it of God? And of God, where for, but to use it with God, and not against him. Seeing then it is not just in God's sight to obey man rather than God . . . kings are instiued to rule in God's fear and laws, as subjects and servants to God, and not against his laws, and above him: it must needs follow (as we first said) that all obedience given to such, wicked princes against God, is playing rebellion in (God's) judgment. And in that case to obey God, and disobey man, is true obedience, how so ever the world judgeth. For as none will condemn Peter and John for (their) disobedience, because they would not herein obey their ordinary magistrates; no more will any which have right

---

[13]*The Works of Thomas Manton*, vol. IV, pp. 327, 328.

judgment, condemn the like resistance in others, which alike is lawful to all. (pp. 60, 61)

Do nothing commanded against God and your conscience, preferring at all times (as you have learned before) the will of God, to the will, punishments, and tyranny of Princes: saying, and answering to all manner of persons: This hath God commanded, this must we do. That hath God forbidded, that we will not do. (p. 116)

When Kings or Rulers become blasphemers of God, oppressors and murderers of thir Subjects, they ought no more to be accounted Kings or lawful Magistrates, but as private men to be examined, accus'd, condemn'd and punisht by the Law of God, and being convicted and punisht by that law, it is not mans but Gods doing. (p. 139)

These are the objections for the most part, or at least the chief (ones), which are commonly alleged against this truth most plain and (self) evident: that is that there is no obedience (to tyrants) to be allowed against God, which is not in His sight disobedience. Also that it is lawful for all men according to their vocation to resist to the uttermost of their power all such as are open enemies of God which labor to make them slaves to Satan. (p. 141)

By the civil laws a foole or Idiot born, and so prov'd shall loose the lands and inheritance wherto he is born, because he is not able to use them aright. And especially ought in no case be sufferd to have the goverment of a whole Nation; But there is no such evil can come to the Commonwealth by fooles and idiots as doth by the rage and fury of ungodly Rulers; Such therfore being without God ought to have no authority over Gods people, who by his Word requireth the contrary. (p. 143, 144)

No person is exempt by any Law of God from this punishment, be he King, Queene, or Emperior, he must die the death, for God hath not plac'd them above others, to trangress his laws as they list, but to be subject to them as well as others, and if they be subject to his laws, then to the punishment also, so much the more as their example is more dangerous. (p. 184)

When Magistrates cease to do their Duty, the people are as it were without magistrates, yea worse, and then God giveth the sword into the peoples hand, and he himself is become immediatly their head. (p. 185)

If Princes do right and keep promise with you, then do you owe to them all humble obedience: if not, you are discharg'd, and your study ought to be in this case how you may depose and punish according to the Law such Rebels against God and oppressors of their Country. (p. 190)

JOHN KNOX (1505–1572)

The story of Knox's life is amazing! Once a slave destined to die in the gallies of a French ship, he converted the nation of Scotland to the Protestant faith and led her to ultimate freedom from tyranny. In respect to political tyranny, Knox stated, "Neither can oath nor promise bind any such people to obey and maintain Tyrants . . . such a one . . . most justly may the same men depose and punish him that unadvisedly before they did nominate, appoint and elect."[14]

In the section below, Knox is confronting "Bloody Mary." He warns her that if she continued in her wicked ways, the people had a right to depose her.

Queen Mary: "Yes, but none of these men raised the sword against their princes."
John Knox: "Yet, Madam, ye cannot deny that they resisted, for those who obey not the commandments that are given, in some sort resist."
Queen Mary: "But yet, they resisted not by the sword?"
John Knox. "God, Madam, had not given them the power and the means."
Queen Mary: "Think ye that subjects, having the power, may resist their princes?"
John Knox: "If their princes exceed their bounds, Madam, no doubt they may be resisted, even by power. For there is neither greater honour, nor greater obedience, to be given to kings or princes, than God hath commanded to be given unto father and mother. But the father may be stricken with a frenzy, in which he would slay his children. If the children arise, join themselves together, apprehend the father, take the sword from him, bind his hands, and keep him in prison till his frenzy be overpast—think ye, Madam, that the children do any wrong? It is even so, Madam, with princes that would murder the children of God that are subjects unto them. Their blind zeal is nothing but a very mad frenzy, and therefore, to take the sword from them, to bind their hands, and to cast them into prison, till they be brought to a more sober mind, is no disobedience against princes, but just obe-

---

[14]*Laing's Knox*, IV, p.539.

dience, because it agreeth with the will of God."

The Queen stormed at the Brethren's freedom of speaking, but she could not amend it; they were of one mind, to maintain the Truth of God and to suppress idolatry. Therefore she began to invent a new craft. She sent for John Knox to come unto her at Lochleven, and she travailled with him earnestly two hours before her supper, that he would be the instrument to persuade the people, and principally the Gentlemen of the West, not to put hands to punish any man for the using of themselves in their religion as please them. The other, perceiving her craft, willed Her Grace to punish malefactors according to the laws, and he durst promise quietness upon the part of all them that professed the Lord Jesus within Scotland. But if Her Majesty thought to elude the laws, he feared some would let the Papists understand that, without punishment, they should not be suffered so manifestly to offend God's Majesty.

"Will ye," quoth she, "allow that they shall take my sword in their hand?"

"The Sword of Justice," quoth he, "Madam, is God's, and is given to princes and rulers for one end, which, if they transgress, sparing the wicked and oppressing innocents, their subjects, who in the fear of God execute judgment, where God hath commanded, offend not God, neither do they sin that bridle Kings from striking innocent men in their rage. The examples are evident:—Samuel feared not to slay Aga, the fat and delicate King of Amalek, whom King Saul had saved. In this case I would earnestly pray Your Majesty to take good advisement, and that Your Grace should let the Papists understand that their attempts will not be suffered unpunished. It shall be profitable to Your Majesty to consider what is the thing Your Grace's subjects look to receive of Your Majesty, and what it is that ye ought to do unto them by mutual contract. They are bound to obey you, and that not but in God: ye are bound to keep laws unto them. Ye crave of them service; they crave of you protection and defence against wicked doers. Now, Madam, if you shall deny your duty unto them, who especially crave that ye punish malefactors, think ye to receive full obedience from them? I fear, Madam, ye shall not."[15]

JOHN MILTON (1608–1674)

Milton is today remembered only as one of the greatest poets in the English language. His best known work is *Paradise*

---

[15]*The History of the Reformation*, pp. 278, 316–317.

Lost. But he was also a knowledgeable theologian and a politician. He wrote in defense of the overthrow and beheading of Charles I. His defense of the right of oppressed people to rise up against cruel tyrants is one of the classics on the subject in the English language. One can easily understand why few people remember this work's title: *The Tenure of Kings and Magestrates: Proving, That it is Lawfull, and hath been held so through all Ages, for any, who have the Power, to call to account a Tyrant, or wicked KING, and after due conviction, to depose, and put him to death; if the ordinary Magestrate have neglected, or deny'd to doe it. And that they, who of late, so much blame Deposing, are the Men that did it themselves.*

In the passages which follow, Milton will refer to various writers in support of his position and will sometimes quote them in Latin. We have not provided a translation of his Latin or updated his old English vocabulary because with historical works of this nature to do so would be to alter the text and make it worthless so far as scholarship is concerned.

> If men within themselves would be govern'd by reason, and not generally give up their understanding to a double tyrannie, of Custom from without, and blind affections within, they would discerne better, what it is to favour and uphold the Tyrant of a Nation. But being slaves within doors, no wonder that they strive so much to have the public State conformably govern'd to the inward vitious rule, by which they govern themselves. For indeed none can love freedom heartilie, but good men; the rest love not freedom, but licence; which never hath more scope or more indulgence then under Tyrants. Hence is it that Tyrants are not oft offended, nor stand much in doubt of bad men, as being all naturally servile; but in whom vertue and true worth most is eminent, them they feare in earnest, as by right their Masters, against them lies all their hatred and suspicion. Consequentlie neither doe bad men hate Tyrants, but have been always readiest with the falsifi'd names of Loyalty, and Obedience, to colour over their base compliances. (p. 1)
>
> For if it needs must be a sin in them to depose, it may as likely be a sin to have elected. And contrary if the peoples act in election be pleaded by a King, as the act of God, and the most just title to enthrone him, why may not the peoples act of rejection, bee as well pleaded by the people as the act

of God, and the most just reason to depose him? So that we see the title and just right of reigning or deposing, in reference to God, is found in Scripture to be all one; visible onely in the people, and depending meerly upon justice and demerit. Thus farr hath bin considered briefly the power of Kings and Magistrates; how it was and is originally the people, and by them conferr'd in trust onely to be imployed to the common peace and benefit; with liberty therefore and right remaining in them to reassume it to themselves, if by Kings or Magistrates it be abus'd; or to dispose of it by any alteration, as they shall judge most conducing to the public good.

We may from hence with more ease, and force of argument determin what a Tyrant is, and what the people may doe against him. A Tyrant whether by wrong or by right comming to the Crown, is he who regarding neither Law nor the common good, reigns onely for himself and his faction: Thus St. Basil among others defines him. And because his power is great, his will boundless and exorbitant, the fulfilling whereof is for the most part accompanied with innumerable wrongs and oppressions of the people, murders, massachers, rapes, adulteries, desolation, and subversion of Citties and whole Provinces. Look how great a good and happiness a just King is, so great a mischeife is a Tyrant; as he the public father of his Countrie, so this the common enemie. Against whom what the people lawfully may do, as against a common pest, and destroyer of mankind, I suppose no man of clear judgment need go further to be guided then by the very principles of nature in him. But because it is the vulgar folly of men to desert their own reason, and shutting their eyes to think they see best with other mens, I shall show by such examples as ought to have most weight with us, what hath bin don in this case heretofore. The Greeks and Romans, as their prime Authors witness, held it not only lawfull, but a glorious and Heroic deed, rewarded publicly with Statues and Garlands, to kill an infamous Tyrant at any time without tryal: and but reason, that he who trod down all Law, should not be voutsaf'd the benefit of Law. Insomuch that Seneca the Tragedian brings in Hercules the grand suppressor of Tyrants, thus speaking,

_____Victima haud ulla amplior Potest, magisque opima mactari Jovi Quam Rex iniquus_____
There can be slaine no sacrifice to God more acceptable Then an unjust and wicked King_____
But of these I name no more, lest it bee objected they were Heathen; and come to produce another sort of men that had the knowledge of true Religion. (pp. 18–19)

LUTHER
Lib. contra Rusticos apud Sleidan.1.5.

Is est hodie rerum status,&c. Such is the state of things at this day, that men neither can, nor will, nor indeed ought to endure longer the domination of you Princes.

Neque vero Caesarem,&c. Neither is Caesar to make Warr as head of Christ'ndom, Protector of the Church, Defender of the Faith; these Titles being fals and Windie, and most Kings being the greatest Enemies to Religion. Lib: De bello contra Turcas. apud Sleid. 1.14. What hinders them, but that we may depose or punish them?

These also are recited by Cochlaeus in his Miscellanies to be the words of Luther, or some other eminent Divine, then in Germany, when the Protestants there entred into solemn Covnant at Smalcaldia. Ut ora ijs obturem &c. That I may stop thir mouthes, the Pope and Emperior are not born but elected, and may also be depos'd as hath bin oft'n don. If Luther, or whoever else thought so, he could not stay there; for the right of birth or succession can be no privilege in nature to let a Tyrant sit irremoveable over a Nation free born, without transforming that Nation from the nature and condition of men born free, into natural, hereditary, and successive slaves. Therfore he saith furder; To displace and throw down this Exactor, this Phalaris, this Nero, is a work well pleasing to God; Namely, for being such a one: which is a moral reason. Shall then so slight a consideration as his happ to be not elective simply, but by birth, which was a meer accident, overthrow that which is moral, and make unpleasing to God that which otherwise had so well pleased him? Certainly not: for if the matter be rightly argu'd, Election much rather then chance, bindes a man to content himself with what he suffers by his own bad Election. Though indeed neither the one nor other bindes any man, much less any people to a necessary sufferance of those wrongs and evils, which they have abilitie and strength anough giv'n them to remove.

Zwinglius.tom.I.articul.42

Quando vero perfide,&c. When Kings raigne perfidiously, and against the rule of Christ, they may according to the word of God be depos'd.

Mihi ergo compertum non est, &c. I know not how it comes to pass that Kings raigne by succession, unless it be with consent of the whole people. ibid.

Quum vero consensu, &c: But when by suffrage and consent of the whole people, or the better part of them, a Tyrant is depos'd or put to death, God is the chief leader in that action. ibid.

Nunc cum tam tepidi sumus, &c. Now that we are so luke warm in upholding public justice, we indure the vices of Tyrants to raigne now a dayes with impunity; justly therfore by them we are trod underfoot, and shall at length with them be punisht. Yet ways are not wanting by which Tyrants may be remoov'd, but there wants public justice. ibid.

Cavete vobis o tyranni. Beware yee Tyrants for now the Gospel of Jesus Christ spreading farr and wide, wil renew the lives of many to love innocence and justice; which if yee also shall do, ye shall be honourd. But if ye shall goe on to rage and do violence, yee shall be trampled on by all men. ibid.

Romanum imperium imo quodq; &c. When the Roman Empire or any other shall begin to oppress Religion, and wee negligently suffer it, wee are as much guilty of Religion so violated, as the Oppressors themselves. Idem Epist. ad Conrad. Somium.

Bucer on Matth.c.5

Si princeps superior, &c. If a Sovran-Prince endeavour by armies to defend transgressors, to subvert those things which are taught in the word of God, they who are in authority under him, ought first to disswade him; if they prevaile not, and that he now beares himself not as a Prince, but as an enemie, and seekes to violate privileges and rights granted to inferior Magistrates or commonalities, it is the part of pious Magistrates, imploring first the assistance of God, rather to try all ways and means, then to betray the flock of Christ, to such an enemy of God: for they also are to this end ordain'd, that they may defend the people of God, and maintain those things which are good and just. For to have supreme power less'ns not the evil committed by that power, but makes it the less tolerable, by how much the more generally hurtful. Then certainly the less tolerable, the more unpardonably to be punish'd.

Of Peter Martyr we have spoke before.

Paraeus in Rom.13.

Quorum est constituere Magistratus, &c. They whose part it is to set up Magistrates, may restrain them also from outragious deeds, or pull them down; but all Magistrates are set up either by Parlament, or by Electors, or by other Magistrates; They therfore who exalted them, may lawfully degrade and punish them.

Of the Scotch Divines I need not mention others then the famousest among them, Knox & and his fellow Labourers in the reformation of Scotland; whose large Treatises on this subject, defend the same Opinion. To cit them sufficiently, were to insert their whole Books, writt'n purposely on this argument. Knox Appeal; and to the Reader; where he promises in a Postscript that the Book which he intended to set forth, call'd, The second blast of the Trumpet, should maintain more at large, that the same men most justly may depose, and punish him whom unadvisedly they have elected, notwithstanding bith, succession, or any Oath of Allegeance. Among our own Divines, Carwright and Fenner, two the Lernedest, may in reason satisfy us what was held by the rest. Fenner in his Book of Theologie maintaining, That they who have power, that is to say a Parlament, may either by faire meanes or by force depose a Tyrant, whom he defines to be him, that wilfully breakes all, or the principal conditions made between him and the Common-wealth. Fen. Sac: Theolog. c. 13. and Carwright in a prefix'd Epistle testifies his approbation of the whole Book.

Gilby de obedientia. p. 25 & 105.

Kings have thir authority of the people, who may upon occasion reassume it to themselves.

England's Complaint against the Canons.

The people may kill wicked Princes as monsters and cruel beasts. (pp. 48–50)

[Here then are the opinions of the] chief of Protestant Divines, we may follow them for faithful Guides, and without doubting may receive them, as Witnesses abundant of what we here affirm concerning Tyrants. And indeed I find it generally the clear and positive determination of them all, (not prelatical, or of this late faction subprelatical) who have writt'n on this argument; that to doe justice on a lawless King, is to a privat man unlawful, to an inferior Magistrate lawfull: or if they were divided in opinion, yet greater then these here alleg'd, or of more authority in the Church, there can be none produc'd. If any one shall go about by bringing other testimonies to disable these, or by bringing these against themselves in other cited passages of thir Books, he will not only faile to make good that fals and impudent assertion of those mutinous Ministers, that the deposing and punishing of a

King or Tyrant, is against the constant Judgement of all Protestant Divines, it being quite the contrary, but will prove rather,
what perhaps he intended not, that the judgement of Divines, if it be so various and inconstant to it self, is not con-
siderable, or to be esteem'd at all. Ere which be yeilded, as I
hope it never will, these ignorant assertors in thir own art
will have prov'd themselves more and more, not to be Protestant Divines, whose constant judgement in this point they
have so audaciously bely'd, but rather to be a pack of hungrie
Churchwolves, who in the steps of Simon Magus thir Father,
following the hot sent of double Livings and Pluralities, ad-
vousons, donatives, inductions, and augmentations, though
uncall'd to the Flock of Christ, but by the meer suggestion of
thir Bellies, like those Priest of Bel, whose pranks Daniel found
out; have got possession, or rather seis'd upon the Pulpit, as
the strong hold and fortress of thir sedition and rebellion
against the civil Magistrate. Whose friendly and victorious
hand having rescu'd them from the Bishops their insulting
Lords, fed them plenteously, both in public and in privat,
rais'd them to be high and rich of poore and base; only suffer'd not thir covetousness & fierce ambition, which as the
pitt that sent out their fellow locusts, hath bin ever bottomless
and boundless, to interpose in all things, and over all persons, their impetuous ignorance and importunity. (pp. 58–
59)

CONCLUSION

We have clearly demonstrated that a solid historical, theological tradition upholds the rights of life, liberty and the
pursuit of happiness as privileges given to all men by their
Creator. The power of government permanently resides in the
people. They may give it to whom they choose and can take
it back when a tyrant arises to oppress them. The right of
Christians to participate in the overthrow of tyranny is upheld
not only as permissible but also as a moral obligation. This
position was embraced by the clearest thinkers in the Christian Church for centuries.

FOR REVIEW AND DISCUSSION

1. When is a government tyrannical? Does the power of the
   state come from the people? Can they take it back when it

is abused by those to whom they had given authority?

2. What clear position prevailed for one thousand years of Church history? What did the best Christian thinkers during this period think of the use of force?

3. What did the Reformers teach about the use of force?

4. When a government becomes tyrannical, what are the steps that the oppressed people should take in order to change the situation?

5. What role did Christians play in the American Revolution?

6

The Creeds and the Confessions

All the churches which came out of the Protestant Reformation, including the Anabaptists, cited scriptural approval of the just use of force by the civil authorities in their confessional standards. They declared the civil government responsible for maintaining social order and defending the nation from its enemies by proper use of force.

The Anabaptists as well as the Lutherans and the Reformed did not hesitate to approve the just use of force. They disagreed whether or not a Christian should be involved with the government or the military.

Most Anabaptists felt that a Christian should not be part of the "world." To them, this meant the government and the military. At the same time, some Anabaptists agreed completely with Christians participating in governmental and military careers.

Many Christians today believe that anyone using force, including the government, is in conflict with the position of historic Christianity, particularly the Anabaptist tradition. This view is erroneous as the following selections from the confessional standards will demonstrate.

The readings which follow contain the original texts of old English creeds. We have neither updated the spelling nor altered the text. We felt compelled to preserve these rare documents. Where the original language was Latin, German or French, we have used the authorized English translation.

THE LUTHERAN STANDARDS

The Larger Catechism (A.D. 1529)

"The government['s] . . . right to take human life is not abrogated. God has delegated his authority of punishing evil doers to civil magistrates. . . . Then what is forbidden here [in the 5th Commandment] applies to private individuals, not to governments." (under the 5th Commandment)

The Augsberg Confession (A.D. 1530)

"It is taught among us that all government in the world and all established rule and laws were instituted and ordained by God for the sake of good order, and that Christians may without sin occupy civil offices or serve as princes and judges, render decisions and pass sentence according to imperial and other existing laws, punish evil doers with the sword, engage in just wars, serve as soldiers, buy and sell, take required oaths, possess property, be married, etc." (ch. XVI)

Summary

Luther made it clear that we are to obey a certain kind of government. The government that God has ordained is a just government which administers good laws. When a government becomes tyrannical, Christians are under no obligation to obey it. Thus Luther stated:

"If the civil magistrate interferes with spiritual matters of conscience in which God alone must rule, we ought not to obey at all."[1]

---

[1] Phillip Schaff, *History of the Christian Church* (Grand Rapids: Eerdmans Publishing Co., 1973), vol. VII, p. 545.

THE REFORMED STANDARDS

The French Confession (A.D. *1559*)

"We believe that God wishes to have the world governed by laws and magistrates, so that some restraint may be put upon its disordered appetites. And as he has established kingdoms, republics, and all sorts of principalities, either hereditary or otherwise, and all that belongs to a just government, and wishes to be considered as their Author, so he has put the sword into the hands of magistrates to suppress crimes." (ch. XXXIX)

The Scottish Confession (A.D. *1560*)

"We confesse and acknawledge Empyres, Kingdomes, Dominionis, and Cities to be distincted and ordained be God; the powers and authoritie in the same, be it of Emperours in their Empyres, of Kingis in their Realmes, Dukes and Princes in the Dominionis, and of utheris Magistrates in the Cities, to be Gods haly ordinance, ordained for manifestatioun of his awin glory, and for the singular profite and commoditie of mankind . . . even the Judges & Princes themselves, to whome be God is given the sword, to the praise and defence of gude men, and to revenge and punish all open malefactors." (art. XXIV)

The Belgic Confession (A.D. *1561*)

"We believe that our gracious God, because of the depravity of mankind, hath appointed kings, princes, and magistrates, willing that the world should be governed by certain laws and policies; to the end that the dissoluteness of men might be restrained, and all things carried on among them with good order and decency. For this purpose he hath invested the magistracy with the sword, for the punishment of evil doers, and for the praise of them that do well." (art. XXXVI)

The Heidelberg Catechism (A.D. 1563)

"Wherefore, also, to restrain murder, the magistrate is armed with the sword." (question 105)

The Thirty-Nine Articles of the Anglican Church (A.D. 1563)

"The laws of the Realm may punish Christian men with death, for heinous and greivous offenses. It is lawful for Christian men, at the commandment of the Magistrate, to wear weapons, and serve in the wars." (art. XXXVII)

The Episcopal Church in America revised the Thirty-Nine Articles in 1801 and added the following to Article XXXVII.

"The Power of the Civil Magistrate extendeth to all men, as well Clergy as Laity, in all things temporal; but hath no authority in things purely spiritual. And we hold it to be the duty of all men who are professors of the Gospel, to pay respectful obedience to the Civil Authority, regularly and legitimately constituted."

The Second Helvetic Confession (A.D. 1566)

"The magistracy . . . is ordained of God himself, for the peace and quietness of mankind. . . . The chief duty of the civil magistrate is to procure and maintain peace and public tranquility. . . . Let him govern the people, committed to him of God, with good laws. . . . Let him exercise judgment by judging uprightly. . . . Let him protect widows, fatherless children, and those that be afflicted, against wrong; let him repress, yea, and cut off, such as are unjust, whether in deceit or violence for he does not bear the sword in vain. And if it be necessary to preserve the safety of the people by war, let him do it in the name of God; provided he hath first sought peace by all means possible, and can save his subjects in no way but by war. And while the magistrate does these things in faith, he serves God with those works that are good, and shall receive a blessing from the Lord." (ch. XXX)

The Irish Articles of Religion (A.D. 1615)

"The supreme government of all estates within the said realms and dominions . . . restrain the stubborn and evil doers with the power of the civil sword." (sec. 57 & 58) In sections 61 and 62, article 37 of the Thirty-Nine Articles is repeated.

The Westminster Confession (A.D. 1647)

"God, the supreme Lord and King of all the world, hath ordained civil magistrates to be under him, over the people, for his own glory and the public good, and to this end hath armed them with the power of the sword, for the defense and encouragement of them that are good, and for the punishment of evil doers.

"It is lawful for Christians to accept and execute the office of a magistrate when called thereunto; in the managing whereof, as they ought especially to maintain piety, justice, and peace, according to the wholesome laws of each commonwealth, so, for that end, they may lawfully, now under the New Testament, wage war upon just and necessary occasion." (ch. XXIII, I, II)

The Savoy Declaration (A.D. 1658)

In this revision of the Westminster Confession, no changes were made in chapter XXIII although chapter XXIV was altered to remove the idea that the civil magistrate had the responsibility to enforce church discipline. The state is to use its force in areas of the common good and not to enforce one particular religion upon the population.

The Sanquhar Declaration (A.D. 1680)

When the tyrannical practices of Charles I were no longer bearable, Scotland rose up in rebellion. The ministers of the church of Scotland were at the very forefront of this revolution. They boldly preached that no scriptural obedience or respect is required toward tyrants. Such governments could be overthrown by the people under the blessing of God.

The following declaration puts into action those principles of freedom which later proved victorious in the Revolution Settlement of 1688. They later resurfaced in the American Revolution of 1776. The major role of Scottish Presbyterians in the American Revolution is directly related to the revolution which took place in Scotland the century before.

"Although we be for government and governors, such as the Word of God and our Covenant allows, yet we for ourselves, and all that will adhere to us, as the representative of the true Presbyterian Kirk and Covenant nation of Scotland, considering the great hazard of lying under such a sin any longer, do by this present disown Charles Stuart, that has been reigning—or rather tyrannising, as we may say—on the throne of Britain these years bygone, as having any right, title to, or interest in the crown of Scotland. We declare that, several years since, he should have been denuded of being king, ruler or magistrate, or having any power to act, or to obeyed as such. We . . . do declare war with such a tyrant and usurper."

Summary

The Reformed confessions are clear in stating that the government which is ordained of God is one that is "regularly and legitimately constituted" (Amer. Revis. Thirty-Nine Articles), i.e., it is a "just government" (the French Confession). Such a government will administer only "wholesome laws" (Westminster Confession), "good laws" (2nd Helvetic Confession). When a government becomes tyrannical, it is no longer ordained of God.

THE ANABAPTIST STANDARDS

The Schleitheim Confession (A.D. 1524)

"We are agreed as follows concerning the sword: the sword is ordained of God. . . . It punishes and puts to death the wicked, and guards and protects the good. In the Law the sword was ordained for the punishment of the wicked and for their death, and the same sword is now ordained to be used by the worldly magistrates." [sixth section]

The Waterland Confession (A.D. 1580)

"Government for the civil Magistrate is a necessary ordinance of God, instituted for the government of common human society and the preservation of natural life and civil good, for the defense of the good and the punishment of the evil." (art. XXXVII)

The Dordrecht Confession (A.D. 1632)

"We also believe and confess, that God has instituted civil government, for the punishment of the wicked and the protection of the pious; and also further, for the purpose of governing the world, countries and cities; and also to preserve its subjects in good order and under good regulations." (art. XIII)

Summary

An examination of the original creeds of the Anabaptists will demonstrate that they accepted the principle of the use of force by civil authorities to punish criminals even unto death. The modern Anabaptists who seek to abolish capital punishment as well as all war would not have been acceptable to the fathers of the original Anabaptist movement.

THE ENGLISH BAPTIST'S STANDARDS

A Short Confession (A.D. 1610)

"Worldly or magistry is a necessary ordinance of God, appointed and established for the preservation of the common estate, and of a good, natural, politic life, for the reward of the good and the punishing of the evil." (sec. 35)

A Declaration of Faith (A.D. 1611)

"That Magistracie is a Holie ordinance off GOD, that every soule ought to bee subject to it not for feare onelie, but for conscience sake. Magistraets are the minsters off GOD for our wealth, they beare not the sword for nought. They are the ministers off GOD to take vengance on them that doe evil. . . . They beare the sword off GOD, —which sword in all Lawful administracions is to bee defended and supported by the servants off GOD that are vnder their Government with their lyves and al that they have." (sec. 24)

The London Confession (A.D. 1644)

"civill Magistracie is an ordinance set up by God for the punishment of evill doers, and for the praise of them that doe well." (ch. XLVIII)

The Somerset Confession (A.D. 1656)

"The ministry of civil justice being for the praise of them that do well, and punishment of evil doers, is an ordinance of God." (ch. XLIV)

The Standard Confession (A.D. 1660)

"We believe that there ought to be civil magistrates in all nations, for the punishment of evil doers, and for the praise of them that do well. . . . Wholesome laws ought to be punished according to the nature of the offenses. . . . If . . . the Civil Powers . . . impose things about matters of religion, which we through conscience to God can actually obey, then we with Peter do say, that we ought in such cases obey God rather than men and accordingly do hereby declare our whole, and holy intent and purpose, that through the help of grace we will not yield, nor in such cases in the least obey them." (sec. XXV)

The Orthodox Creed (A.D. 1678)

"The supreme lord and king of all the world, hath ordained civil magistrates to be under him, over the people for his own glory, and for the public good. And the office of a magistrate, may be accepted of and executed by Christians, when lawfully called thereunto; and God hath given the power of the sword, into the hands of all lawful magistrates, for the defense and the encouragement of them that do well, and for the punishment of evil doers, and for the maintenance of justice, and peace, accordingly to wholesome laws of each kingdom, and commonwealth, and they may wage war upon just and necessary occasions." (art. XLV)

CONCLUSION

Our survey of the original documents of the churches that came out of the Reformation has demonstrated that Protestants as well as Roman Catholics believed in the just use of force by the civil authorities. It is also equally clear that if a government is tyrannical and its laws are oppressive, it has divested itself of God's ordination. Such a government can be resisted and disobeyed with the blessing of God.

The present-day members of such mainline denominations as the Lutheran, Presbyterian, Reformed, Episcopal, Methodist, Brethren, and Baptist churches should not sell their spiritual birthright by accepting the modern pacifist idea that the use of force at any time by anyone, including the state, is morally and intrinsically evil. Even the fathers of the Anabaptists clearly understood that without the coercive power of force, society itself would be destroyed by anarchy. They would agree that total disarmament would lead to society's destruction as oppressors would freely trample on the weak. We hope that the modern heirs of the Reformation return to their spiritual roots and embrace this aspect of the faith of their fathers.

FOR REVIEW AND DISCUSSION

1. Does your church have a creed or confession of faith? What does it say about the power of the state, war, capital punishment and related issues?

2. What three movements arose from the Reformation?
3. Did all the original creeds of the three forces of the Reformation recognize the need for the state to use force?
4. What position did all the Reformation creeds take concerning capital punishment?
5. Discuss the following statement: "It is morally right for a non-Christian to protect my family, but it would be morally wrong for me to protect them."

Francis Schaeffer and Other Modern Leaders

In this chapter we have gathered statements made by various influential evangelical leaders in the twentieth century. These leaders openly defend the biblical use of just force in the context of modern times. We have included these readings to bring the issues and arguments up to date and to demonstrate that the historic theology of the Christian Church will always have its loyal and able defenders.

LORAINE BOETTNER

Boettner is one of the most influential writers in the twentieth century whose books have found their way into virtually every minister's library.

As the storm clouds of the Third Reich began to cast their shadow over Europe in the late 1930s, the Nazis launched a massive "peace" campaign as part of their program of conquest.

As part of this program, it was essential that the Nazis get the churches involved in calling for disarmament and reductions in military spending. Thus various church officials began to call for "peace" at any price. They were convinced that if the Allies, and America in particular, dared to go to war against Hitler's military might, the destruction would be so terrible that civilization itself would return to the Dark Ages. Pacifism became their only hope of survival.

As Hitler's troops began to invade the nations lying on their borders, these leaders urged a policy of concession in which Hitler would be allowed to grab one country at a time. They sincerely believed that the Nazis didn't really want to conquer the world. They would stop after taking a few countries and Europe would remain safe.

In this context, Boettner wrote *The Christian Attitude Toward War*. It is interesting to point out that his descriptions of Nazi Germany are exact parallels to the Soviet Union now. The following quote could have been written yesterday concerning the Soviets instead of forty years ago about Nazi Germany.

> Within the space of a few short years we have witnessed the rise of the dictator nations, imbued with the idea that war is heroic, and equipped with great military power which they do not hesitate to use ruthlessly. Their whole economy has been reorganized for the sole purpose of waging successful wars. Their persistent policy of armed aggression has already resulted in the stamping out of numerous small nations and the practical inslavement of millions of human beings. (p. 12)[1]

Boettner's response to the pacifists of his day can be easily applied to modern pacifists. We again quote from *The Christian Attitude Toward War*:

> We want to be neither pacifists, nor militarists. We would define a pacifist as one who will not sanction or take part in any war no matter what the occasion or the apparent justification—one who is for peace at any price; and we would define a militarist as one who favors heavy military armaments, primarily for purposes of aggression against other nations. We expect to show that the position which should be taken by anyone who is a true Christian and also a loyal citizen lies somewhere between these two extremes.
>
> It should hardly be necessary to say that we hate war as do all right-minded people. We hope that our country may never have to engage in another. We desire peace, but we realize there are some things worse than war. We desire peace, but not the kind that is found in the cemetery or in the slave

---

[1]Loraine Boettner, *The Christian Attitude Toward War* (Grand Rapids: William B. Eerdman's Publishing Company, 1942).

camp. It is true that Christ came as the Prince of peace, and that His followers should strive to promote peace by all lawful means. And for that reason it may seem strange that any professed Christian should enter a protest against the modern pacifist movement. Anyone who does speak against it, or against certain trends in it, doubtless will be misunderstood by some. We believe, however, that that movement is dangerous, and that it has no necessary or legitimate part in the evangelical Christian program. (pp. 10, 11)

JOHN MURRAY (1898–1975)

Murray is considered by some as being the greatest Reformed theologian of the twentieth century. Generations of his students at Westminster Seminary in Philadelphia would probably agree. After developing the biblical principles which apply to human government, Murray goes on to point out:

It is in the light of these principles that we are to view the power of the sword vested in the civil magistrate. It is a strange turn of thought which causes some who espouse an evangelical view of Holy Scripture to fail to appreciate the implications of the biblical teaching that the powers that be are ordained of God to bear the sword and execute wrath upon evildoers (cf. Romans 13:1–7; 1 Peter 2:13–17). It is true, of course, that all punishment is evil; for all punishment is the wages of sin. But it does not follow that the execution of the evil which consists in punishment is per se sinful. If this were so then God himself would commit sin in executing wrath, a blasphemous thought. And it cannot be gainsaid that God appoints agents who are the instruments in the execution of his wrath who unholily and wickedly fulfil his holy and righteous purpose (cf. Isaiah 10:5–14). But God also appoints ministers with the commission to be the executors of punishment with the result that they are obliged to put the penalty into effect. It is this kind of appointment that the civil magistrate has received; he is responsibly the minister of God. He is not only the means decreed in God's providence for the punishment of evildoers—something that may be said of every instrument, however bad, which executes the divine retribution—but he is God's instituted, authorized, and prescribed instrument for the maintenance of order and the punishment of evildoers.

This conception of the magistrate's authority, so distinctly enunciated in the biblical passages cited above, reveals the weakness of the pacifist contention. Paul says that the civil magistrate is the minister of God, an avenger for wrath upon him who does evil, that he attends upon the service committed to him, and that it is for this reason that, out of conscience toward God, we must be in subjection. It is as the avenger of evildoing and in pursuance of that function that he bears the sword (Roms. 13:4–6). And Peter puts the matter no less clearly when he says that governors are sent by the Lord for vengeance on evildoers (1 Peter 2:14). The sum of this teaching is that, when the civil magistrate executes just judgment upon the crimes committed within the sphere of his jurisdiction, he is executing not simply God's decretive will, he is not merely the providential instrument of God's wrath, but he is actively fulfilling the charge committed to him, and it would be a violation of God's preceptive will not to do so. And what is true in respect of his prerogative within his domain applies also to any attempt from without, by aggression or otherwise, to upset the order of justice and peace which it is his commission to maintain. When one state, for example, unjustly wages war on another, resistance on the part of the state which is the victim of aggression is nothing more than the application of the same principle in terms of which the civil magistrate executes justice upon the violators of equity, order, and peace, within his own domain. By what kind of logic can it be maintained that the magistrate, who is invested with the power of the sword (Roms. 13:4) may and must execute vengeance upon evildoers within his domain but must sheath the sword of resistance when evildoers from without invade his domain? When he resists this attempt from without to disrupt the order which it is his duty to maintain, he must do this by his appointed agents, the forces which are armed with the sword. To plead pacifism or non-resistance under such conditions is to annul the New Testament teaching that the civil magistrate is sent by the Lord to punish and suppress evildoing and to maintain the order of justice, well-doing, and peace. The institution of civil government is not totalitarian. But within its own well-defined sphere of jurisdiction, it exists for the maintenance and promotion of well-being that we may lead a quiet and peaceable life (cf. 1 Timothy 2:21). In a word, it is for the purpose of preserving and promoting "life." It is the principle of the sanctity of life that undergirds this institution, and its punitive functions no less than the more positive find their sanction in that sanctity.[2]

---

[2]John Murray, *Principles of Conduct* (Grand Rapids: Eerdmans Publishing Co., 1968), pp. 114, 115.

GLEASON ARCHER

At this time, Dr. Archer is a professor at Trinity Evangelical Seminary. His careful scholarship and cogent defense of the integrity of the Bible as the Word of God have made him an internationally known and respected scholar of the highest caliber. What follows is his answer to a question concerning the goodness of God and the wars He commanded in the Old Testament.

How could a good God, a God of peace, condone warfare (1 Chron. 5:22), give instructions as to how war should be fought (Deut. 20), and be acclaimed by His people as "the Lord is a warrior"? (Exod. 15:3)

The key element in 1 Chronicles 5:22 which tells of the tribal conquests of Reuben, Gad, and Manasseh over the pagan races of Transjordan is: "For many fell slain, because the war was of God."

Underlying this question are certain assumptions that require careful examination as to their soundness. Is it really a manifestation of goodness to furnish no opposition to evil? Can we say that a truly good surgeon should do nothing to cut away cancerous tissue from his patient and simply allow him to go on suffering until finally he dies? Can we praise a police force that stands idly by and offers no slightest resistance to the armed robber, the rapist, the arsonist, or any other criminal who preys on society? How could God be called "good" if He forbade His people to protect their wives from ravishment and strangulation by drunken marauders, or to resist invaders who have come to pick up their children and dash out their brains against the wall?

No policy would give freer rein to wickedness and crime than a complete surrender of the right of self-defense on the part of the law-abiding members of society. No more effective way of promoting the cause of Satan and the powers of hell could be devised than depriving law-abiding citizens of all right of self-defense. It is hard to imagine how any deity could be thought "good" who would ordain such a policy of supine surrender to evil as that advocated by pacifism. All possibility of an ordered society would be removed on the abolition of any sort of police force. No nation could retain its liberty or preserve the lives of its citizens if it were prevented from maintaining any sort of army for its defense. It is therefore incumbent on a "good God" to include the right of self-defense as the prerogative of His people. He would not be good at all if He were to turn the world over to the horrors of unbridled cruelty perpetrated by violent and bloody criminals or the unchecked aggression of invading armies.

Not only is a proper and responsible policy of self-defense taught by Scripture from Genesis to Revelation, but there were occasions when God even commissioned His people to carry out judgment on corrupt and degenerate heathen nations and the complete extermination of cities like Jericho (cf. the article on "Was Joshua justified in exterminating the population of Jericho?" in connection with Joshua 6:21). The rules of war laid down in Deuteronomy 20 represented a control of justice, fairness, and kindness in the use of the sword, and as such they truly did reflect the goodness of God. Special hardship conditions were defined as a ground for excusing individual soldiers from military duty until those conditions were cleared up (Deut. 20:5–7). Even those who had no such excuse but were simply afraid and reluctant to fight were likewise allowed to go home (v.8). Unlike the heathen armies, who might attack a city without giving it an opportunity to surrender on terms (cf. 1 Sam. 11:2–3; 20:1–2), the armies of Israel were required to grant a city an opportunity to surrender without bloodshed and enter into vassalage to the Hebrews before proceeding to a full-scale siege and destruction. Even then, the women and children were to be spared from death and were to be cared for by their captors (Deut. 20:14). Only in the case of the degenerate and depraved inhabitants of the Promised Land of Canaan itself was there to be total destruction; a failure to carry this out would certainly result in the undermining of the moral and spiritual standards of Israelite society, according to vs. 16–18. (This corrupting influence was later apparent in the period of the Judges [Judg. 2:2–3,11–15]).

In the New Testament itself, the calling of a soldier is considered an honorable one, if carried on in a responsible and lawful fashion (Matt. 8:5; Luke 3:14; Acts 10:1–6, 34–35). Paul even uses the analogy of faithful service in the army as a model for Christian commitment (2 Tim. 2:4), without the slightest suggestion of reproach for military service. In a similar vein is the description in Ephesians 6:11–17 of the spiritual armor to be put on by the Christian warrior in the service of his Lord. There does not appear to be any basis in Scripture, either in the Old Testament or the New, for the concept of a "good" God who enjoins pacifism on His followers.[3]

---

[3]Taken from *Encyclopedia of Bible Difficulties*, pp. 219, 220, by Gleason L. Archer, Jr. Copyright © 1982 by The Zondervan Corporation. Used by permission.

FRANCIS SCHAEFFER (1912–1984)

If we were asked to name a modern Christian leader that has changed the course of the evangelical church in his own generation, Francis Schaeffer would be the obvious choice. He has done something that we never thought possible. He has awakened the sleeping giant of Fundamentalism to its social, political and national obligation to be involved in applying the lordship of Christ to abortion and other crucial issues which face us today. His position on war and pacifism comes from his adopted Scottish Presbyterian heritage.

The following quotes are from his work *A Christian Manifesto:*

> There does come a time when force, even physical force, is appropriate. The Christian is not to take the law into his own hands and become a law unto himself. But when all avenues to flight and protest have closed, force in the defensive posture is appropriate. This was the situation of the American Revolution. The colonists used force in defending themselves. Great Britain, because of its policy toward the colonies, was seen as a foreign power invading America. The colonists defended their homeland. As such, the American Revolution was a conservative counter-revolution. The colonists saw the British as the revolutionaries trying to overthrow the legitimate colonial governments.

> A true Christian in Hitler's Germany and in the occupied countries should have defied the false and counterfeit state and hidden his Jewish neighbors from the German SS Troops. The government had abrogated its authority, and it had no right to make any demands. (pp. 117–118).

> The Founding Fathers, in the spirit of Lex Rex, cautioned in the Declaration of Independence that established goverments should not be altered or abolished for "light and transient causes." But when there is a "long train of abuses and usurpations" designed to produce an oppressive, authoritarian state, "it is their right, it is their duty, to throw off such government . . . ."

> Simply put, the Declaration of Independence states that the people, if they find that their basic rights are being systematically attacked by the state, have a duty to try to change that government, and if they cannot do so, to abolish it. (p. 129)

> It is time we consciously realize that when any office com-

mands what is contrary to God's Law it abrogates its authority. And our loyalty to the God who gave this law then requires that we make the appropriate response in that situation
to such a tyrannical usurping of power. I would emphasize
at this point that Samuel Rutherford was not wrong, he was
right; it was not only in the seventeenth century in Scotland
where he was right; it was not only in 1776 where he was
right: He is right in our century. (pp. 131–132)[4]

Dr. Schaeffer has also written *Who Is for Peace?*, from which
the following quotes are taken:

Unilateral disarmament in this fallen world, especially in
the face of aggressive Soviet materialism with its anti-God
basis, would be altogether utopian and romantic. It would
lead, as utopianism always does in this fallen world, to disaster. (p.26)
. . . what should be our own perspective on military pre-
paredness? . . . From my own study of Scripture I would say
that to refuse to do what I can for those who are under the
power of oppressors is nothing less than the failure of Christian love. . . . This is why I am not a pacifist. Pacifism in this
poor fallen world in which we live—this lost world—means
that we desert the people who need our greatest help. (p.
23)[5]

Conclusion

The clearest thinkers and the most biblically sound Christians in every age have seen the justice of using force in personal and civil defense. While doing nothing to stop evil has
always led to greater evil, the just use of force has allowed
free societies to exist and true religion to flourish. Christianity
and tyranny can never be reconciled because Christ, not the
state, is the Lord of all of life.

FOR REVIEW AND DISCUSSION

1. What historical parallels do you see between the so-called
   "peace" movements started by the Nazis just before WW

---

[4]From *A Christian Manifesto* by Dr. Francis Schaeffer, copyright © 1981, pages
117, 129, 131, 132. Used by permission of Good News Publishers/Crossway
Books, Westchester, Illinois 60153.
[5]Dr. Francis Schaeffer with Vladmir Bukovsky and James Hitchock, *Who Is for
Peace?* (Nashville: Thomas Nelson Publishers, 1983).

II and the present day "peace" movements?

2. Did the appeasement of Hitler and the disarmament treaties made with him help prevent or lead to war? What can be said about present day attempts to appease the Communists? Will they help prevent war?

3. What is the government's responsibility toward its citizens according to Dr. John Murray?

4. How can God be called "the God of war" if He is a God of Love?

5. What is the Christian's responsibility according to Francis Schaeffer?

8

Questions and Answers

The following is a summary of some of the questions which have been posed to us. They represent the sincere questions of people who come from a humanistic or religious pacifist background.

Honest questions deserve an honest answer. Therefore, we will attempt to answer them without offending anyone. Given the emotional nature of some of the issues and questions, we hope the reader will remember that what we say is said in love.

PHILOSOPHICAL QUESTIONS

Question: Isn't the taking of a human life always wrong regardless of the circumstances?

Answer: While the above question is a clear expression of a sincere belief, sincerity is not enough to establish its truthfulness. Merely stating something does not prove it.

When we turn to the Scriptures we find that God himself takes human life (1 Sam. 2:6). God's taking of human life can be on a massive scale, as with the Flood, or as individual judgment (Acts 5:1–11).

As the image-bearer of God, man is called upon to take human life in certain circumstances such as a punishment for murder (Ex. 21:12; Luke 20:9–16).

Since human life is a gift of God, it can be withdrawn by God's command. In the Bible, God has directed the taking of human life in such circumstances as criminal justice or war. Those who take human life in such circumstances are merely acting as the agents of God. This is why the government officials who use the sword to punish evildoers are called the "ministers of God" in Rom. 13:4.

Question: Isn't human life sacred? Then it would be wrong to destroy it.

Answer: Human life is not sacred in and of itself. Only in reference to God and His Word is human life elevated above animal life. Because man is created in the image of God, the sin of murder must result in the greatest punishment possible, which is the just taking of the murderer's life. Thus, the sacredness of life forms the basis of capital punishment (Gen. 9:6).

Question: While a case can be made for some wars in the past being just, how can nuclear war which will annihilate all life ever be justified?

Answer: First, if one admits that wars in the past were fought for valid and just reasons, then these same reasons may well justify war which involves nuclear weapons. What is moral and right *in principle* does not change because of circumstances.

Second, the real underlying argument goes like this: If nuclear war will destroy all life on the earth, then this kind of war is not just because it is not winnable or survivable. It would be better to surrender to the Soviets and live as a slave under tyranny than to participate in such a war.

Christians need to understand that there is not conclusive scientific evidence that all life would be destroyed on this planet if nuclear war broke out. Since this question concerns a future possibility that has never happened before, it is pure speculation that all life would end.

One of the recent arguments that has been used by Carl

Sagan and other pacifists is the idea of a "nuclear winter" in which the temperature of earth would remain below freezing for 200 years because the dust and ash in the atmosphere after nuclear explosions would prevent the sun from warming up the earth. Of course, all life on earth would be destroyed.

The National Academy of Sciences decided to look into this theory and found that the worst that would happen after nuclear war would be a brief drop in temperature for at most twenty weeks. If this happened in July, the temperature would drop to 55° in Kansas. This is a far cry from the 200 years of freezing temperature claimed by the pacifists. The so-called "nuclear winter" is just another "better red than dead" scare tactic.[1]

As a matter of historical record, the "doomsday myth" was invented to scare people into a "better red than dead" position. The pacifist literature is filled with the use of such scare tactics as a propaganda tool.

Many scientists believe that nuclear war is not only survivable but winnable. Every person who has been frightened by the doomsday myth should read *Nuclear War Survival Skills*[2] in order to hear both sides of the issue.

If speculating about the future is a valid way to prove your position, then we would like to offer a proposition. If the Free World disarmed and surrendered to the Communists, given the fact that they have killed over 150 million people in this century, and have recently slaughtered half the population of Cambodia, then more deaths would probably result after the Communists took over than would die in a nuclear war! The holocaust of death which would follow disarmament would no doubt exceed any horror that any war ever produced.

Another vital point, God's Word guarantees that humanity will *not* be annihilated by wars of its own making. Jesus said that the earth would continue to experience wars until He returned to judge the wicked. (Matt. 24:6).

In this light, it is shameful for Christian pacifists to use the

---

[1]*The Review of the News* (Jan. 23, 1985) pp. 49, 50.
[2]*Nuclear War Survival Skills* (Aurora, Ill.: Caroline House Pub., 1980).

doomsday myth as a "scare tactic" to convert people to pacifism. Contradicting the Word of the God they claim to believe in, they tell us the only choices before us are either nuclear war, which will destroy "all life on the planet," or giving up our "anti-communism and myopic anti-Sovietism" by surrendering to the tyranny of the Soviets.[3] This is the tactic used in such popular pacifist books as Ron Sider's *Nuclear Holocaust & Christian Hope* and *Perspectives In Peacemaking.*

Some leaders have begun to push openly for a "Better red than dead" ideology. We cannot help but recall those theologians who unwittingly helped the Third Reich in its military conquests because of their "Better Nazi than dead" ideology. The millions who died in battle and in the death camps demonstrate where such thinking leads.

We should also recognize that the Soviet's entire military strategy is built upon the concept of a winnable nuclear war.[4] Since they view nuclear war as something they could not only survive but win, the only realistic position the West can take is to approach it in the same way.

Question: Would not pacifism and nonviolent forms of resistance best safeguard our lives? Shouldn't we give peace a chance by signing disarmament agreements with the Soviets?

Answer: Historical evidence rises up against such an idea. For example, the European Jews' attachment to pacifism and nonviolent resistance made them easy targets for acts of violence for centuries. This reached its climax with the death of six million Jews in Nazi concentration camps.

Modern Jews have learned this lesson well. Their cry "Never Again!" is eloquent testimony that while pacifism can provoke violence, military strength will deter it.

The pacifist model was historically tried out by the Jews. It ended in staggering death tolls over the centuries, probably much higher than would have resulted if they had taken up arms to defend themselves.

---

[3] John A. Bernbaum, ed., *Perspectives on Peacemaking* (Ventura, Calif.: Regal Books, 1984), p. 182.
[4] Viktor Suvaron, *Inside the Soviet Army* (New York: Macmillan, 1982).

At the cost of over one million dollars, a team of historians examined all the disarmament agreements that have occurred in the last one thousand years of Western history. They found that in every recorded instance, the disarmament agreements led to war.

The "honest" side that actually disarmed was without exception attacked by the "dishonest" side, and usually conquered. In the past, disarmament agreements have always given aggressors military superiority while placing peace-seeking nations in a state of fatal weakness.[5]

HISTORICAL QUESTIONS

Question: Isn't it true that all the early Christians were pacifists until Constantine?

Answer: Many pacifists assume that the early church was pacifist. Ron Sider in *Perspectives on Peacemaking* states with dogmatism:

> Until the time of Constantine in the fourth century, all Christian writing reflects the belief that Jesus clearly and explicitly forbade Christians to participate in war and capital punishment. (p.140)

What is astounding to us is that Sider does not give us any proof for his position that "all" the writers in the early church openly spoke out against war, military participation and capital punishment!

Mr. Sider and others like him do not attempt to document their position by citations from the early Fathers because such citations do not exist. If "all" the writings of the early church "clearly" and "explicitly" taught pacifism, there should be hundreds of citations in support of this. Why has no one ever found them?

We demonstrated in Chapter 4 that the early Christian Fathers never uttered one word of condemnation of war *per se*, and the majority of the Fathers had no problems with Christians participating in just wars or capital punishment.

---

[5]*The Review of the News* (Dec. 26, 1984) pp. 53–54.

Sider and other pacifists have ignored the historical evidence and have overstated their case.

Question: Didn't the horrors of the Thirty Years' War during the Reformation reveal that pacifism would have been a better way?

Answer: There is not a single example of a Protestant church which survived during the Reformation that did not require taking up arms to defend its religious freedom. Even the early Anabaptists took up arms when they were in the majority, as in The Peasants' War.[6]

Foxes' Book of Martyrs records the annihilation of those churches which did not defend themselves or have someone else defend them.

The "peace" churches exist today because of the military victory of the reformers. The Pope's armies would not have left the Anabaptists in peace once they had defeated the reformers in battle. A holocaust of death would have surely followed.

When Cromwell's diplomatic efforts to lessen the persecution of Protestants in Catholic countries such as Italy and France failed, he threatened to invade Europe with his army of godly psalm-singing puritans to punish the Catholics for murdering Protestants. Persecution ceased in many places.[7]

Question: What about Gandhi's successful use of nonviolent resistance?

Answer: Richard Grenier in *The Gandhi Nobody Knows*,[8] Saul Alinsky in *Rules for Radicals*[9] and George Orwell's *Reflections on Gandhi* all present historical evidence that Gandhi was a pacifist only when it served his purposes.

They demonstrate that the British were not driven out by

---

[6]Norman Cohn, *The Pursuit of the Millennium* (New York: Oxford University Press, 1970).
[7]Robert Paul, *The Lord Protector: Religion and Politics in the Life of Oliver Cromwell* (Grand Rapids: Eerdmans Publishing Co., 1955).
[8]Richard Grenier, *The Gandhi Nobody Knows* (Nashville: Thomas Nelson, 1983).
[9]Saul Alinsky, *Rules for Radicals* (St. Paul: Vintage Book Co., 1972).

Gandhi's hunger strikes or by peaceful demonstrations, but by the violence which attended such things. Gandhi's so-called pacifism was successful only because he was dealing with a democratic Christian nation. Even Gandhi admitted that his tactics would not work in totalitarian states.

BIBLICAL QUESTIONS

Question: Doesn't the Old Testament concept of "shalom" (i.e., peace) necessarily involve the idea that all war is evil?

Answer: The Old Testament authors had no problem with gaining and preserving *shalom* or peace by the use of force, even by war. Thus 2 Sam. 11:7 (literal Hebrew) could speak of "the *shalom* of the soldiers" and "the *shalom* of the war." In Josh. 21:43–44, Israel gained "rest" through military victory. It is thus biblically inaccurate to say that the Old Testament concept of shalom excludes the concept of war.

Question: The Old Testament looked forward to the time when the Messiah would cause swords to be beat into plowshares and spears into pruning hooks (Isa. 2:4). The lion and the lamb would lie down together. All wars would cease and shalom, or peace, would cover the earth.
Since this Kingdom is now established on earth by Christ, isn't it our responsibility to resist all the use of force in all contexts? We must destroy all our weapons to fulfill the biblical prophecies.

Answer: The earthly kingdom which Christ ushers in by His literal and personal return to this world (Zech. 14:3–5) will result in a new heaven and a new earth where righteousness and shalom reign because the wicked have been removed and sent into eternal punishment (Matt. 25:46).

At that time, the effects of Adam's sin will be removed from nature itself (Rom. 8:19–22) as the children of God are manifested by their resurrection from the dead (Rom. 8:11, 18–25).

This glorious kingdom of peace is a living "hope" according to Paul in Rom. 8:24. Since it is a "hope," this means that we do *not* have it already, "for who hopes for what he already has? If we hope for what we do not yet have, we wait for it patiently" (Rom. 8:24–25).

Since Christ has not yet returned and the wicked have not yet been removed, wars will continue (Matt. 24:6–8). As long as the wicked remain, governments must use force to control them. When Jesus returns and sets up His glorious kingdom, there will be no need of force for He shall reign with divine authority.

Question: The just-war theory utilizes the Old Testament as its foundation. Isn't this wrong since Christians should base their lives on the teaching of Jesus?

Answer: The unity of the Scriptures should not be broken simply because we don't like what they say. The New Testament authors did not hesitate to derive doctrine and ethics from principles contained in the Old Testament (2 Tim. 3:16–17).

Furthermore, when pacifists think they have found something in the Old Testament to back up their position, such as "shalom," they use it without hesitation. They end up doing what they condemn others for doing!

For example, when arguing against the just-war theory, Ron Sider states that the Old Testament proves "too much" and "too little" to be of any practical use.[10] But when Sider argues for a form of socialism in which wealth is redistributed by force, he bases his argument on over 150 Old Testament quotations.[11]

Evidently, the use of the Old Testament is valid only as long as it is used to promote socialism. But as soon as the Old Testament is used to strengthen the West's moral resolve to defend its freedoms with force if necessary, pacifists like Sider reply that the Old Testament cannot be used. Do only socialists have the right to use the Old Testament?

---

[10]Ronald Sider and Richard Taylor, *Nuclear Holocaust and Christian Hope* (Downers Grove, Ill.: InterVarsity Press, 1982), pp. 138–140.

[11]Ronald Sider, *Rich Christians in an Age of Hunger* (Downers Grove, Ill.: InterVarsity Press, 1977).

Question: Since by His nonviolent life Jesus revealed that He was a pacifist, shouldn't we follow His example? After all, He did not join the army or fight in any wars.

Answer: The money-changers in the temple would have trouble with the idea that Jesus was nonviolent. They remember His whip with which He drove them out of the temple (John 2:12–17).

Jesus' use of divine force in self-defense to guarantee that no one could take His life except at the appointed time forever justifies self-defense (John 18:4–6; Luke 4:28–29).

Jesus did not judge sinners at His first coming because He came to accomplish salvation (John 3:17). At His second coming He will use force to inflict eternal punishment upon the wicked (Matt. 25:46).

Jesus' unique mission of salvation excluded Him from many normal things in life, such as marriage, following a career, owning a home or fighting in a war. Obviously, we are not called to follow Jesus' example in all these things. It is not logically valid to say that we are not to do something simply because Christ did not do it in His lifetime.

Question: Didn't John the Baptist and Jesus teach that it was wrong to use violence?

Answer: In Luke 3:14, John the Baptist gives the soldiers three commands: "Don't extort money and don't accuse people falsely—be content with your pay." Nowhere does John the Baptist condemn the occupation of soldier *per se.*

Nowhere did Jesus in the Gospel record tell the state to disarm, or that it is wrong for a nation to maintain a police or military force, or that Christians should not participate in political or military careers.

Question: Doesn't the Bible say, "Thou shalt not kill"?

Answer: The Hebrew word *murr* in Ex. 20:13 means "murder" and not simply killing. This is why the NIV, the NKJV, the NASB and many other modern translations translate it, "You shall not *murder.*"

The very next chapter establishes that murderers should be put to death (Ex. 21:12). The Ten Commandments condemn the unauthorized taking of human life.

Question: Since Jesus calls us to be "peacemakers," shouldn't we join the modern "peace" movements?

Answer: Dr. Clarence Macartney wisely warned in his own generation:

> Before Christians commit themselves to pacifist movements, they do well to ascertain whether these movements rise out of a genuine aversion to war or whether they are part of a scheme to disarm the country and render it incapable of resisting the machinations of those who would overthrow its historic institutions.[12]

There is no longer any doubt whatsoever of the truth that many of the so-called "peace" movements are either funded, directed or manipulated by the Soviet KGB. The documentation for this is so clear and overwhelming that it is found in secular sources (both liberal and conservative), such as *The New York Times* (4/17/1977), the *Reader's Digest* (8/1982), *Human Events* (12/4/1983; 1/8/1983), *The Wall Street Journal* (5/10/1982), *Newsweek* (5/6/83). The evidence is also clear in Christian books, such as *The Church and the Sword, Who Is for Peace?* and *Bad News for Modern Man*.[13]

We do not feel that it is "unkind" to point out the truth just because it hurts (Gal. 4:16). Christians need to be realistic and not romantic about the modern "peace" movements. These groups will lead us into war if they disarm the Free World. They are not really for peace but actually have a "death wish" as documented in *Bad News for Modern Man*.

We must remember that the Nazis used the "peace" movements in their day to destabilize and disarm the West in order to secure an easy victory over the Allied powers.[14]

---

[12]G.R. Evans and C.C. Singer, *The Church and the Sword* (Houston: St. Thomas Press, 1982), p. 1.

[13]Franky Schaeffer, *Bad News for Modern Man* (Westchester, Ill.: Crossway Books, 1984), pp. 23–26.

[14]*American Spectator*, 3/1983.

Another favorite method of the Nazis to prepare a country for easy takeover was to disarm the population by strict gun control. If the people did not have weapons in their homes, they could do nothing to resist an invasion.

Is it any wonder that gun control is a part of the agenda of the present-day "peace" movements? In West Germany alone, in one year, the Soviets gave over 30 million dollars to finance the "peace" party.[15] Such evidence can no longer be waved aside by sincere pacifists, Christian or humanist.

Lenin always viewed pacifism as a weapon. He said:

> When a country is selected for attack, we must first set before the youth a mental barrage which will forever prohibit the youth from being molded into an armed force to oppose our invading armies. This can most successfully be done by creating 'war horror' thought and by the teaching of pacifism and non-resistance.[16]

The Soviets still have the same method in mind. This is clear from this comment made by Aleksei Ivanovich Rykov, a past president of the Council of Commissioners of the U.S.S.R.:

> It is our duty to inculcate in the minds of all nations, the theories of international friendship, pacifism, and disarmament, encouraging resistance to military appropriations and training, at the same time, however, never for one moment relaxing our efforts in the upbuilding of our military establishment.[17]

Moscow certainly backs demonstrations in Europe over the deployment of U.S. missiles. These so-called "peace" or "green" groups have never seen anything wrong with the *Soviet* deployment of missles that has been going on for years. Only N.A.T.O. is condemned for setting up a strong defense network.

These facts do not mean that every Christian or humanist who supports pacifism does so because Moscow orders it. Many sincere individuals, out of reasons of conscience, do not

---

[15]*Newsweek*, 5/6/83.

[16]G.R. Evans and C.C. Singer, *The Church and the Sword* (Houston: St. Thomas Press, 1982), p. 11.

[17]*Rules and Governments of the World*, Vol. 3 (Bowker Pub., 1972), 521, 522.

believe in the use of force. We have no problem honoring their good motives in this regard. We hope they will examine the truth of what we are saying for their own good. They need to if they wish to maintain the freedom to believe as they choose.

Question: Do you feel that America is God's country in the same way as Israel was in the Old Testament?

Answer: It would hardly be proper to give any country status that belongs only to Israel or to the church. We are Christians first and our ultimate allegiance is to Christ's kingdom (Phil. 3:20). America or any other nation will be blessed by God if they follow those principles in God's Word which describe the functions of a just government. However, no nation is to be viewed as a divine theocracy on earth.

Question: Is it proper to use the Old Testament when it relates only to the theocracy of Israel?

Answer: We have sought to examine the morality of using force throughout Israel's history in the Old Testament. This history includes the experiences of God's people both before and after the theocracy. That which is moral will be moral in any age. Since the use of force was approved in all the ages before and after the theocracy, the use of force is not something unique to the theocratic kingdom.

Question: How can a Christian participate in war when he may be called upon to do covert activities such as spying? After all, we must tell the truth even to our enemies.

Answer: The just-war theory does not condone the idea that "anything goes" in wartime. Cromwell's army was called "Holy Ironsides" because they did not rape and plunder like the typical armies of their day. They marched into battle under the banner of the Lord because they were "puritan" in their lives as well as in their doctrines.

John Murray discusses covert activity and the right to conceal the truth from our enemies in *Principles of Conduct*. He concludes that the Bible does not teach that we owe the truth to everyone at all times, including our enemies. Ethics' experts like Erickson point out that wartime calls for special rules.[18]

According to Proverbs, a wise man does *not* tell everything he knows (Prov. 10:19; 13:3; 17:27, 28; 21:23; 29:11). Someone who tells everyone what he knows is guilty of gossip, slander, and breaking confidences.

Concealing the truth by refusing to answer someone's questions or simply by not saying anything is perfectly proper because it is not the same as lying. To think that God would condemn concealing things from one's enemies is absurd. This would make biblical ethics impractical and unlivable.

In the Old Testament, both Moses and Joshua sent spies into enemy territory under the direction and blessing of God (Num. 13; Josh. 2). Whatever God commands cannot be viewed as morally wrong unless one believes that God is the author of evil.

Joshua's spies entered Jericho, where they were concealed by Rahab from enemy soldiers (Josh. 2). She is exalted as an example of courage and faith by the author of Hebrews (11:31). She is not condemned for hiding the spies.

If it were morally wrong to be involved in covert activities, why was Rahab blessed and not cursed? How can concealment be wrong when God himself planned Israel's ambush at Ai by having Joshua conceal his troops (Josh. 8:2)?

In the New Testament, we have the example of none other than the spotless Son of God. In John 7:1–10, His half brothers taunted Him by saying that He should go up to Jerusalem and publicly demonstrate that He was the Messiah (v. 4). Jesus told them in verse 8 that He was not going up to Jerusalem. Then in verse 10, we are told that Jesus went *secretly* up to Jerusalem! Yet we know Jesus did not "lie" to His brothers.

Or again, when Jesus stood before the civil authorities, He refused to answer their questions because He was not under any moral obligation to tell them anything (Matt. 27:1–14). The Apostle Paul used a covert rescue operation to escape his enemies (Acts 9:25).

---

[18]Millar Erickson, *Relativism in Contemporary Christian Ethics* (Grand Rapids: Baker Book House, 1974), p. 149ff.

When we turn to church history, we find that such godly men as Calvin and Knox used false names to escape their enemies. Corrie Ten Boom and others concealed Jews from the Nazi exterminators during the war. The underground churches in Communist countries have to use covert operations just to meet for worship. If they told the KGB the names of all their fellow believers and where they met because they were under the delusion that they were bound by the Bible to tell the truth to everybody, including their enemies, millions of them would have been destroyed years ago.

The Bible is once again shown to be practical and relevant even in the "sticky" situations that international problems and war creates. God's law never calls upon us to do what is insane or stupid. "His commandments are not burdensome" (1 John 5:3).

CONCLUSION

The above questions are some of the most frequently asked by our pacifist friends. We have also attempted to present those questions which are raised in the pacifist literature on the subject. We should never be afraid to ask honest questions. They will ultimately lead us to the Truth if we search the Scriptures with an open mind (John 7:17).

Conclusion

History has demonstrated that the greatest foe of tyranny is biblical Christianity. Totalitarian states cannot allow the free preaching of the Gospel because Christ is proclaimed as the Lord over all of life, including the state. This means that the state cannot do as it pleases. The state may not design its own "morality" as it goes along. The state itself must answer to a higher power one day.

Given these truths, what practical steps should we take?

1. *Gather information.* There are now dozens of good books to read, tapes to listen to, films to see and video tapes to study. (See our bibliography for recommendations.)

2. *Absorb the knowledge.* Think about it. Turn it over in your mind until light dawns and you see clearly what is going on today and what the Bible tells you to do about it. Be informed about the issues facing us now and the possible problems in the future.

3. *Seek out others.* At church and at work, begin to talk about what you are reading. You will be surprised to see how many of your friends will come "out of the woodwork" because they too have been worried about the same things that bother you. They have not said anything because they thought you were not concerned.

4. *Pool your information.* Share with your friends the books, tapes, etc., you have and they will share with you. Keep each other informed.

5. *Organize a discussion group.* We know of families that have rented all the Schaeffer films to show in their living room for their family and friends. Start a "book of the month club" in your church and sponsor good books. Take a Sunday school class and teach your students about their biblical responsibility to oppose tyranny.

6. *Get involved.* Write letters to the editors of newspapers and magazines when you find them pushing the tyranny of abortion, disarmament, etc. Call up the late night talk shows and let them hear the truth for a change. Visit your local TV station and get on their local talk shows. It is a lot easier than you think. If they have a "speak out" program, then get on the program and speak out about relevant issues. Write, phone and visit your local and federal politicians. Join a political party and work to see its platform reflect biblical concerns such as the need for a strong military to defend your country. Go on marches and demonstrations. Register people to vote. Give your money to support good causes.

One quick way to find practical things to do where you live is to join one or more of the Christian action groups. Groups such as the Moral Majority, The Roundtable, Christian Voice, and Freedom Foundation will be more than happy to give you responsibility if you want to become active in applying the lordship of Christ to all of life. They have newsletters which will keep you informed of what is happening. If there isn't a Christian political action group near you, then start your own local organization. You can do plenty of things in your town or neighborhood. You can buy space in local newspapers and "penny savers" and do your own editorials. It may cost you only the price of a meal.

7. *Be prepared.* Don't be caught unprepared for any natural or man-made disaster. We do not recommend anyone becoming a "survivalist." However, it is just common sense to keep your home supplied with extra food and other supplies against the chance of flood or famine. Your church should have a "food bank" to help people in the community.

8. *Train your children.* Give them good role models and heroes to follow such as missionaries or Reformation heroes

whose Christianity was strong, aggressive and virile. Teach them that their greatest loyalty should be to Christ and His kingdom. Constantly tell that God is the ultimate Judge of all. Create a theistic environment for them in your home by talking about scriptural truths—when you are getting up in the morning or getting ready for bed, when you are relaxing in your home or riding in the car (Deut. 6:7).

9. *Be willing to suffer*. If you are going to resist the powers of darkness, it is going to cost you. You must freely give your money, time and energy to do Christ's work. You will get tired and discouraged. People may say unkind things about you. Others will not understand why you are so concerned. Satan will attack you at your weakest point.

"Therefore, my dear brothers, stand firm. Let nothing move you. Always give yourselves fully to the work of the Lord, because you know that your labor in the Lord is not in vain" (1 Cor. 15:58).

To do nothing to oppose evil is a great evil in itself. Benjamin Franklin warned people in his own day: "Man will ultimately be governed by God or by tyrants."[1]

Is it too much to expect people in this modern world to die if necessary for what they believe? More Christians have been killed for their faith in the twentieth century than in all the centuries before.[2] Shall we be carried to heaven "on flowery beds of ease, while others fight to win the prize and sail through bloody seas"?

Martin Luther answered these questions in his own day by these words:

> A mighty fortress is our God, a bulwark never failing;
> Our helper he amid the flood of mortal ills prevailing;
> For still our ancient foe doth seek to work us woe;
> His craft and power are great; and armed with cruel hate,
> On earth is not his equal. . . .
> The prince of darkness grim, We tremble not for him;

---

[1]Quoted in *They Preached Liberty*, by Franklin P. Cole (Orem, Utah: Liberty Press, 1979), intro.

[2]James & Marti Hefley, *By Their Blood: Christian Martyrs in the 20th Century* (Milford, Mich.: Mott Media, 1979), intro.

> His rage we can endure, for lo his doom is sure;
> One little word shall fell him. . . .
> Let goods and kindred go, this mortal life also;
> The body they may kill; God's truth abideth still;
> His kingdom is forever.
> Amen.

May God raise up millions like Martin Luther who saw no sacrifice too great to be made in the cause of God and Truth. To God be the glory!

Recommended Reading

Those books marked by an asterisk (*) are recommended reading for those who love freedom.

A Nation Under God? ed. C.E. Gallivan. Waco, Texas: Word Books, 1976.

Adams, R. *The Better Part of Valor*. University of Washington Press, 1962.

Ahlstrom, Samuel. *A Religious History of the Armenian People*. Yale University Press, 1972.

Alinsky, Saul. *Rules for Radicals*. Vintage Books, 1972.

Aquinas, Thomas. *Summa Theologica*. New York: McGraw-Hill Book Co., vol. 35, pp. 81–93.

*Archer, Gleason. *Encyclopedia of Bible Difficulties*. Grand Rapids: Zondervan Pub. Co., 1982.

Argee, L. *A History of Armenian Christianity*. American Missionary Assoc., 1946.

Atlya, A. *A History of Eastern Christianity*. London: Melhuen & Co. Ltd., 1968.

Augustine. *City of God*. Harvard University Press, n.d.

Bainton, Roland H. *Christian Attitude Toward War and Peace*. Nashville: Abingdon, 1960.

Balke, Willem. *Calvin and the Anabaptist Radicals*. Grand Rapids: Wm. B. Eerdmans Pub. Co., 1981.

Beachey, D. *Faith in a Nuclear Age*. Scottdale, Penn.: Herald Press, 1983.

Bernbaum, John A., ed. *Perspectives on Peacemaking*. Ventura, Calif.: Regal Books, 1984.

Billington, James. *Fire in the Minds of Men: Origins of the Revolutionary Faith*. New York: Basic Books, 1980.

*Boettner, Loraine. *The Christian Attitude Toward War*. Grand Rapids: Eerdmans, 1942.

Brock, Peter. *Pacifism in the United States: From Colonial Era to the First War*. Princeton University Press, 1968.

_____. *Twentieth-Century Pacifism*. Reinhold: Van Nostrand, 1970.

Brown, Dale W. *Brethren and Pacifism*. Elgin, Ill.: Brethren Press, 1970.

*Brutus, Junius. *A Defense of Liberty Against Tyrants*. (1689) Massachusetts: Peter Smith, 1963.

*Bundy, Edward. *How Liberals and Radicals Are Manipulating Evangelicals*. Wheaton Ill.: Church League of America, 1982.

Butterfield, Harold. *Christianity, Diplomacy and War*. New York: Abingdon-Cokesbury Press.

Cadoux, C. *Christian Pacifism Re-Examined*. Garland Pub., 1972.

Cadoux, C. *The Early Christian Attitude to War*. London: George Allen, 1919.

*Calvin, John. *Institutes of the Christian Religion*. Philadelphia: Westminster Press, 1967, (IV, XX).

*Campbell, Douglass. *The Puritan in Holland, England, and America*. Vols. 1, 2. New York: Harper & Row, 1892.

*Clark, Gordon. *What Do Presbyterians Believe?* Philadelphia: Pres. & Ref. Pub. Col. 1965.

Classical Armenian Culture. University of Pennsylvania: Samaelian Scholars Press, 1982.

**Collected Writings of John Murray*. Edinburgh: Banner of Truth Trust, 1976, vol. 1, pp. 47ff. "God and War."

*Cohn, Norman. *The Pursuit of the Millennium*. Oxford University Press, 1970.

Cole, Franklin P. *They Preached Liberty*. Orem, Utah: Liberty Press, 1976.

Craige, Peter. *The Problem of War in the Old Testament*. Grand Rapids: Eerdmans, 1978.

Cyclopedia of Biblical, Theological and Ecclesiastical Literature.

Grand Rapids: Baker Book House, 1981, "War."

*D'Aubigne, J. *History of the Reformation*. New York: American Tract Society, 1848, 5 vols.

————. *The Protector: A Vindication*. (1861) Harrisonburg, Virginia: reprinted by Sprinkle Pub., 1984.

*Dabney, Robert. *Lectures in Systematic Theology*. Grand Rapids: Zondervan, 1972, pp. 401ff.

*DeMar, Gary. *God and Government*. Georgia: American Vision Press, 1982.

Diehl. *Inscriptions Latinae Christinae*. Berlin, 1925–1931.

*Denny, James. *War and the Fear of God*. Hodden, 1916.

Donaldson, James and Alexander Roberts, ed. *Ante-Nicene Fathers*, vols. 1–5. Grand Rapids: Eerdmans, 1981.

*Douglas, Ann. *The Feminization of American Culture*. New York: Avon Books, 1977.

Douglass, James. *The Non-Violent Cross*. Riverside, N.J.: Macmillan Company, 1968.

Drinan, Robert. *Vietnam and Armageddon*. New York: Scribner's Sons, 1970.

Dymond, J. *An Inquiry into the Accordance of War with the Principles of Christianity*. Wood & Co., 1876.

Eddy, S., and K. Page. *The Abolition of War*. Doran Col., 1924.

Edwards, G. *Jesus and the Politics of Violence*. New York: Harper & Row Pub., 1972.

*Ellul, Jacques. *Violence: Reflections from a Christian Perspective*. Seabury, 1969.

*Erickson, Millard. *Relativism in Contemporary Christian Ethics*. Grand Rapids: Baker Book House, 1974.

Eusebius's Ecclesiastical History. Grand Rapids: Baker Book House, 1981.

*Evans, G.R., and C.C. Singer *The Church and the Sword*. Box 35046, Houston, Tex.: St. Thomas Press, 1982.

Fletcher, Joseph. *Situation Ethics*, Philadelphia: The Westminster Press, 1966.

French, P. *We Won't Murder*. Hastings House, 1940.

*Frend, W. *Martyrdom and Persecution in the Early Church*. Grand Rapids: Baker Book House, 1965.

*Gillespe. *Aaron's Rod Which Budded*. (n.d.).

Gilson, Etinne. *The Philosophy of Saint Augustine*. New York: Vantage Books, 1967.

Greaves, Robert. *Theology and Revolution in the Scottish Reformation*. Grand Rapids: Eerdmans, 1980.

*Greene, William. "The Christian Doctrine of War." *Princeton Theological Review*, XVI, 81, Jan. 1918.

*_____. "War Neither Absolutely Right nor Absolutely Wrong in Itself." *Princeton Theological Review*, XVI, 642, Oct. 1918.

*Grenier, Richard. *The Gandhi Nobody Knows*. Nashville: Thomas Nelson, 1983.

Guinness, Os. *Violence*. Downers Grove, Ill.: InterVarsity Press, 1979.

*Harnack, Adolph. *Militia Christi*. Philadelphia: Fortress Press, 1946.

Harris, Douglas. *The Biblical Concept of Peace: Shalom*. Grand Rapids: Baker Book House, 1970.

Harris, Robert and Jerry Paxman. *A Higher Form of Killing*. New York: Hall & Wang, 1982.

Heering, G.J. *The Fall of Christianity*. New York: Fellowship Pub., 1928.

*Hefley, James and Marti. *By Their Blood: Christian Martyrs of the 20th Century*. Milford, Mich.: Mott Media, 1979.

*Helgeland, J. "Christians and the Roman Army A.D. 173–337." *Church History*, vol. 43, 1974.

*Hennecke, Edgar. "Gospel of Thomas." *New Testament Apocrypha*. Vol. 1, 2, ed. Wilhelm Schneemelcher. Philadelphia: The Westminster Press, 1963.

*Henry, Carl. *Christian Personal Ethics*. Grand Rapids: Baker Book House, 1957.

Hershberger, Guy. *War, Peace and Nonresistance*. Scottdale, Penn.: Herald Press, 1944.

*Hocker, E. *The Fighting Parson of the American Revolution*. Philadelphia, 1936.

*Hodge, Archibald. *The Confession of Faith*. London: The Banner of Truth Trust, 1964.

*Hodge, Charles. *Systematic Theology*. London: James Clark & Co., 1960, vol. 3, pp. 365ff.

*Hughes, Phillip. *Theology of the English Reformers*. Grand Rapids: Eerdmans, 1965.

*Hollander, Paul. *Political Pilgrims*. New York: Oxford University Press, 1981.

*Holmes, Arthur. *War and Christian Ethics*. Grand Rapids: Baker Book House, 1975.

Hornus, Jean. *It is Not Lawful for Me to Fight: Early Christian Attitudes Towards War, Violence, and the State*. Scottdale, Penn.: Herald Press, 1980.

International Standard Bible Encyclopedia. ed. J. Orr. Grand Rapids: Eerdmans, 1939.

Johnson, J. *The Meaning of War*. Old Tappan, N.J.: Fleming Revell, 1939.

Kahn, H. *On Thermonuclear War*. Princeton University Press, 1960.

Kearney, Cresson. *Nuclear War Survival Skills*. Aurora, Ill.: Caroline House, 1981.

*Kik, Marcus. *Church and State*. New York: Thomas Nelson & Sons, 1963.

Kingdom, David. *The Gospel of Violence*. Pasadena: Carey Pub., n.d.

Kirkemo, Ronald. *Between the Eagle and the Dove*. Downers Grove, Ill.: InterVarsity Press, 1970.

*Knox, John. *The History of the Reformation of Religion Within the Realm of Scotland*. Carlisle, Penn.: Banner of Truth, 1982.

Lasserre, J. *War and Peace*. Scottdale, Penn.: Herald Press, 1962.

*Lee, U. *The Historic Church and Modern Pacifism*. New York: Abingdon-Cokesbury Press, 1943.

Lenski, R. *The Interpretation of St. Matthew's Gospel*. Minneapolis, Minn.: Augsburg, 1933.

Lightfoot, J.B. *Apostolic Fathers*. Part 2, vol. 1. Grand Rapids: Baker Book House, 1889, reprinted in 1981.

Lindsell, Harold. *The Armageddon Spectre*. Westchester, Ill.: Crossway Books, 1985.

*Locher, G. *Zwingli's Thought*. Leiden, 1981.

Macky, Peter. *Violence*. Waco, Tex.: Word, 1973.

McClintock, John and James Strong. *Cyclopedia of Biblical, The-*

ological and Ecclesiastical Literature. Vol. 5. Grand Rapids: Baker Book House, 1981.

MacGregor, G. *The New Testament Basis of Pacifism and the Relevance of an Impossible Ideal.* New York: Fellowship Pub., 1960.

*McIntire, Carl. *The Rise of the Tyrant.* Christian Beacon Press, 1945.

*Meeter, Henry. *The Basic Ideas of Calvinism.* Grand Rapids: Kregel Pub., 1956.

Meyer, F. *In Defense of Freedom.* Chicago: Regency, 1962.

*Moffatt, James. "War," *Dic. of Apo. Church,* 1918, vol. 2, p. 607ff.

Morrison, C. *The Christian and War.* New York: Willett, Clark & Co., 1942.

*Murray, John. *Principles of Conduct.* Grand Rapids: Eerdmans, 1968.

*Musurillo, Herbert. *The Acts of the Christian Martyrs: Texts and Translations.* Oxford University Press, 1972.

*Nash, Ronald. *Social Justice and the Christian Church.* Milford, Mich.: Mott Media, 1983.

*Neibuhr, Reinhold. *Christian Realism and Political Problems.* New York: Scribner's Sons, 1953.

_____. *Moral Man and Immoral Society.* New York: Scribner's Sons, 1932.

Nersurjan, H. *A History of the Armenian Church.* Armenian Church of North America, 1963.

New Catholic Encyclopedia. Vol. 14, Catholic University of America, 1967.

Nuclear War: What's in It for You? New York: Pocket Books, 1982.

Nuclear War Survival Skills. Aurora, Ill.: Caroline House Pub., 1980.

Papajian, S. *A Brief History of Armenia.* 1976.

*Paul, Robert. *The Lord Protector: Religion and Politics in the Life of Oliver Cromwell.* Grand Rapids: Eerdmans, 1955.

Poling, D. *A Preacher Looks at War.* New York: Macmillan, 1943.

Preston, Richard. *Can We Disarm?.* Toronto: Canadian Institute of International Affairs, 1958.

*Purves, Jock. *Fair Sunshine*. London: Banner of Truth Trust, 1965.

*Ramsey, Paul. *The Just War: Force and Political Responsibility*. New York: Scribner & Sons, 1968.

*Ramsey, William. *Luke the Physician and Other Studies in the History of Religion*. Grand Rapids: Baker Book House, 1979.

Raven, Charles. *The Theological Basis of Christian Pacifism*. New York: Fellowship Pub., 1950.

————. *War and the Christian*. New York: Macmillan, 1938.

*Reid, William. "Calvin and Political Order" in *John Calvin: Contemporary Prophet*. Philadelphia: Pres. & Ref. Pub. Co., 1959.

Rifken, Jeremy and Ted. *The Emerging Order*. New York: G. P. Putnam's Sons, 1979.

*Rushdooney, Rousas. *The Institutes of Biblical Law*. New Jersey: The Craig Press, 1973.

*Russell, E. "John Knox as Statesman." *Princeton Theological Rev.*, VI, I, Jan. 1908.

*Rutherford, Samuel. *Lex Rex*. Harrisonburg, Va.: Sprinkle Pub., 1982.

*Ryan, E. "The Rejection of Military Service by the Early Church." *Theo. Stud.*, 13, March 1952.

Saint Thomas Aquinas: Philosophical Texts. New York: Oxford Univer. Press, 1960.

*Schaeffer, Francis. *A Christian Manifesto*. Westchester, Ill.: Crossway Books, 1981.

*————. *The Great Evangelical Disaster*. Westchester, Ill.: Crossway Books, 1984.

————. Vladimir Bukovsky and James Hitchock, *Who Is For Peace?* Nashville: Thomas Nelson Pub., 1983.

*Schaeffer, Franky. *Bad News for Modern Man*. Westchester, Ill.: Crossway Books, 1984.

*Schaff, Phillip. *History of the Christian Church*. Grand Rapids: Eerdmans, 1973.

Sherwin-White, A. *Roman Society and Roman Law in the New Testament*. Grand Rapids: Baker Book House, 1981.

*Shields, William. ed. by J. Howe. *Faithful Contendings Displayed*. Geosglow, 1780.

*Shields, A. *A Hind Let Loose*. 1687.

Sider, Ronald and Richard Taylor. *Nuclear Holocaust & Christian Hope*. Downers Grove, Ill.: InterVarsity Press, 1982.

*Singer, C. *The Unholy Alliance*. New York: Arlington House, 1975.

*Smellie, Andrew. *Men of the Covenant*. London: Banner of Truth Trust, 1962.

Smith, W. *Calvin's Ethics of War*. Annapolis, Md.: Academic Fellowship, 1972.

*Solzhenitsyn, Aleksander. *East & West*. New York: Harper & Row, 1972.

*_____. *The Mortal Danger*. New York: Harper & Row, 1980.

*Suvaron, Viktor. *Inside the Soviet Army*. New York: Macmillan, 1982.

The Causes of War. ed. A. Porritt. New York: Macmillan, 1932.

The Christian and the State in Revolutionary Times. The Westminster Conference, 1975.

The Christian and War. Historic Peace Churches, 1958.

The Complete Writings of Menno Simons. Scottdale, Penn.: Herald Press, 1974.

The Encyclopedia of Philosophy. ed. Paul Edwards, New York: Macmillan, 1907.

The Morality of War. Pontifico Universitas Lateranenses Academia Alfonsiana, 1970.

The Puritan Ethic in United States Foreign Policy. ed. Larson. New York: D. Van Nostrand Co., 1966.

The Recovery of the Anabaptist Vision. ed. Hershberger. Scottdale, Penn.: Herald Press, 1957.

The Theology of Christian Resistance: Christianity & Civilization. ed. Gary North. Geneva Divinity School Press, 1983.

The Works of Ezekiel Hopkins. Philadelphia, Pa.: Leighton Pub., 1874.

The Works of Hidreich Zwingli. New York: Putnam's Sons, 1912.

The Works of Robert Hall. New York: Harper & Row, 1839.

Van Prenster, Guillaume. *Unbelief and Revolution*. Amsterdam, 1975.

Walzer, Michael. *Just and Unjust Wars*. New York: Basic Books, 1977.

_____. *Revolution of the Saints: A Study in the Origins of Radical Politics*. New York: Atheneum, 1968.

War: Four Christian Views. ed. Robert Clouse. Downers Grove, Ill.: InterVarsity Press, 1981.

War, Peace and Violence. International Bibliography 1973–1974, Cerdic Pub., 1975, No. 18.

Walton, R. *Zwingli's Theocracy*. University of Toronto Press, 1967.

Wertham, Frederic. *A Sign for Cain*. New York: Macmillan, 1966.

*Whitehead, John W. *The Second American Revolution*. Elgin, Ill.: David C. Cook Pub., 1982.

*_____. *The Stealing of America*. Westchester, Ill.: Crossway Books, 1983.

*Williamson, G.I. *The Westminster Confession of Faith for Study Classes*. Philadelphia: Pres. & Ref. Pub. Co., 1964.

*Wirt, Sherwood. *The Social Conscience of the Evangelical*. New York: Harper & Row, 1968.

*Wollebius, Johannes. *Compendium Theologica Christianae*. Bk. 11, Ch. X in *Reformed Dogmatics*. ed. Beardslee, III. New York: Oxford University Press, 1965.

Yoder, E. *Must Christians Fight*. The Mennonite Central Committee, 1943.

Yoder, J. *Karl Barth and the Problem of War*. Nashville: Abingdon Press, 1970.

Yoder, John. *Peace Without Eschatology*. Scottdale, Penn.: Mennonite Pub. House, 1954.

_____. *The Original Revolution*. Scottdale, Penn.: Herald Press, 1971.

_____. *The Politics of Jesus*. Grand Rapids: Eerdmans, 1972.

Zahn, G. *An Alternative to War*. New York, 1963.

Zwingli and Bullinger. Lib. of Christian Classics, XXIV.